P9-CDX-122

ALSO BY *Graham Blackburn*

Illustrated Housebuilding

The Illustrated Encyclopedia of
Woodworking Handtools, Instruments
& Devices

Illustrated Basic Carpentry

The Postage Stamp Gazetteer

Illustrated Furniture Making

Illustrated Interior Carpentry

The Illustrated Encyclopedia of
Ships, Boats, Vessels, and other
water-borne Craft

The Illustrated Dictionary of
Nautical Terms

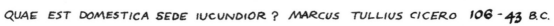

QUAE EST DOMESTICA SEDE IUCUNDIOR ? MARCUS TULLIUS CICERO 106 - 43 B.C.

THE PARTS
OF A HOUSE

ILLUSTRATED AND
DESCRIBED BY

GRAHAM BLACKBURN

RICHARD MAREK PUBLISHERS · NEW YORK

copyright © 1980 by G.J. Blackburn

All rights reserved. No part of this book may be reproduced in any form or by any means without the prior written permission of the Publisher, excepting brief quotes used in connection with reviews written specifically for inclusion in a magazine or newspaper. For information write to

Richard Marek Publishers, Inc.
200 Madison Avenue
New York, New York
1 0 0 1 6

LIBRARY OF CONGRESS CATALOGING IN PUBLICATION DATA

Blackburn, Graham, 1940-
    The parts of a house.

    1. House construction — Dictionaries.
I.   Title.
TH4812.B52   690'.03'21   80-382
ISBN 0-399-90074-8

Designed by Graham Blackburn

Printed in the United States of America

102958

BELMONT COLLEGE LIBRARY

TH
4812
.B52

DEDICATED WITH GRATITUDE
TO THE MEMORY OF

Holley Cantine

1916 - 1977

REQUIESCAT IN PACE

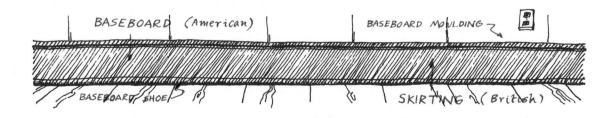

PREFACE

This book is an attempt to take apart and describe the constituent parts of a typical, one or two family house. Everyone is familiar with door and floor, but what lies behind the door or under the floor is for many of us a mystery.

I have tried to explain, in the most general terms, a building's basic anatomy; but just as no two people are exactly alike, so are houses seldom identical, although many may share a similar framework and have been constructed on similar principles. Therefore your mullions and muntins may not be quite as I have drawn them, but the chances are that you will have some, and will be able to recognize them from what is written here.

Also, while I have tried to include everything that might be part of a house's construction, not everything here will be found in a single house — so you may look in vain for your cricket or cornice return, but you will know them when you see them on another house.

Almost everybody lives in a building of some kind, and while this book refers specifically to smaller houses, much of the information is pertinent to dwellings in general, including flats, apartment buildings, and institutional residences. (However, it must be borne in mind that the reverse is not necessarily true; there are some features of very large buildings not mentioned here.)

I hope that for those who own, rent, build, or simply stay in a house, this book will help in understanding the building that surrounds them, and thereby increase their ability to appreciate it, maintain it, repair it, and simply to enjoy it.

Finally, I would like to express my gratitude to two people who are responsible for this book: my father, John Blackburn, who, as I was about to build my first house, offered me the then obscure advice, "don't forget to corbel your eaves and parge your flues!" (this book is partly the result of my attempt to plumb the meaning of those mysterious words); and Elaine Chabach, who introduced me to my Publishers and thus made this book a reality.

Graham Blackburn
THE CROWN AND ANCHOR
W O O D S T O C K
NEW YORK   1979

1 0

THE PARTS OF A HOUSE

THE WHITE KING WATCHING THE CARPENTERS   a woodcut by WEISSKUNIG, 1515

ANCHOR BOLT

Anchor bolts are long bolts cemented into the top of a foundation wall, and to which the sill of a wood-frame house is bolted, thereby securing the house to its foundation.

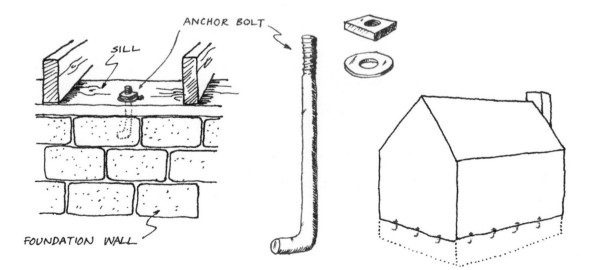

APRON

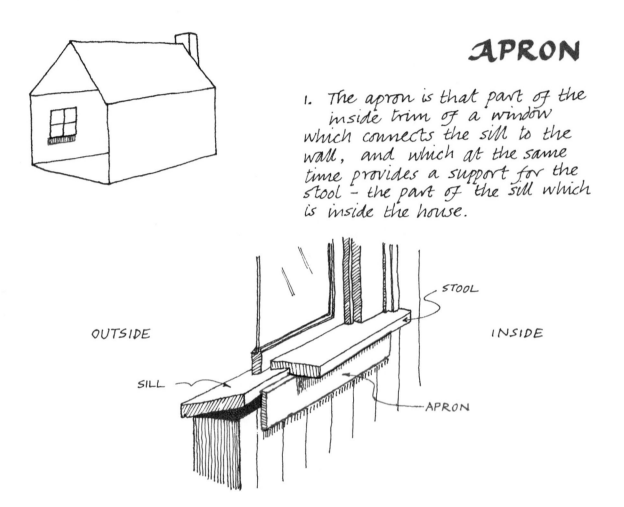

1. The apron is that part of the inside trim of a window which connects the sill to the wall, and which at the same time provides a support for the stool - the part of the sill which is inside the house.

OUTSIDE

INSIDE

STOOL

SILL

APRON

2. The term apron is also applied to a paved area at the juncture of a driveway with a garage or the street.

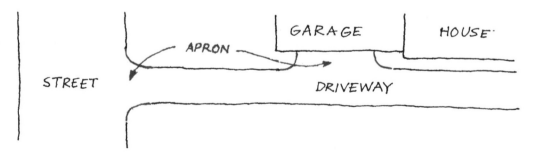

GARAGE   HOUSE

APRON

STREET

DRIVEWAY

ARCHITRAVE

Although in classical architecture architrave refers to the bottom section of an entablature – the part of the building above the columns – in common usage it refers to the moulded frame surrounding a door or a window.

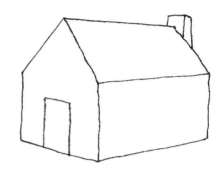

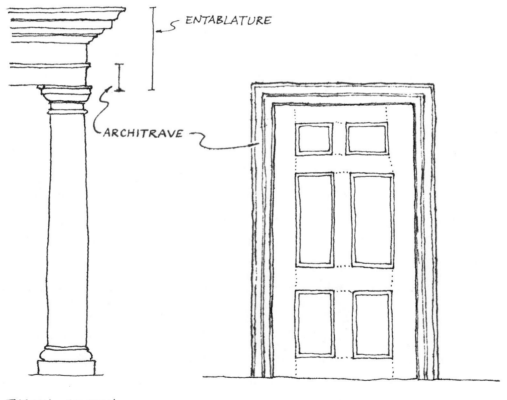

ENTABLATURE

ARCHITRAVE

TUSCAN COLUMN

SIX-PANEL DOOR

ASH DUMP

An ash dump is that part of a fireplace hearth which may be opened to allow the ashes from the fire to fall through into a pit below the hearth. The ashpit is a more convenient place to store ashes until their removal than the hearth itself.

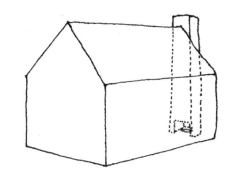

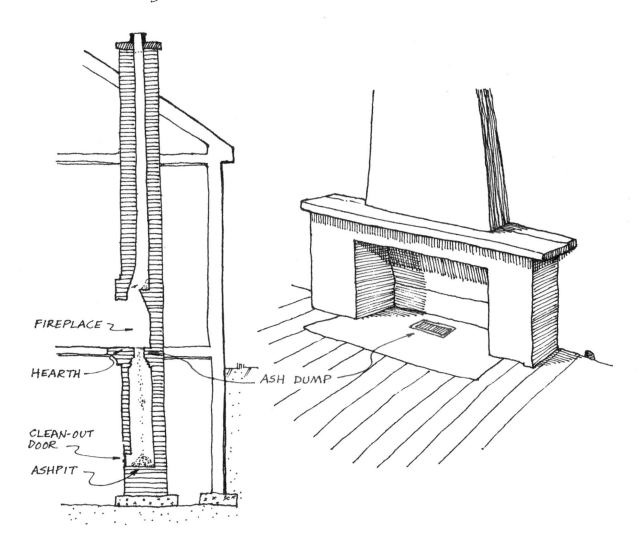

FIREPLACE

HEARTH

ASH DUMP

CLEAN-OUT DOOR

ASHPIT

ATTIC

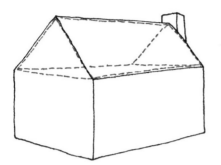

The room or space in the roof of a house is called the attic — provided there is a room below.

Attic has an interesting origin, for it takes us all the way back to Ancient Greece. Athens was the capital of Attica, and being famous for its architecture, Attic came to mean pure in style, and gave its name to a small order (a column and entablature) built above a much larger order. This smaller order – the Attic Order – often enclosed another room or storey of the building which became known as the Attic Storey. Since the Attic Storey was the topmost, when the orders disappeared, the upper storey, in the roof of a building, was called simply the Attic.

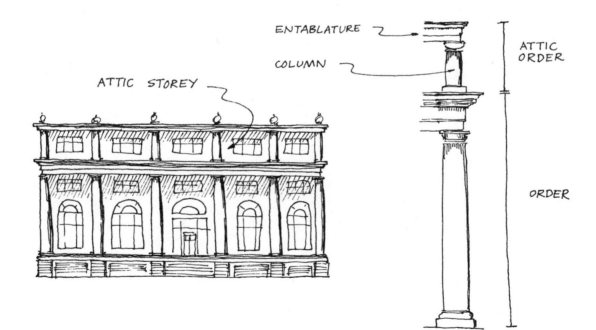

ATTIC STOREY

ENTABLATURE

COLUMN

ATTIC ORDER

ORDER

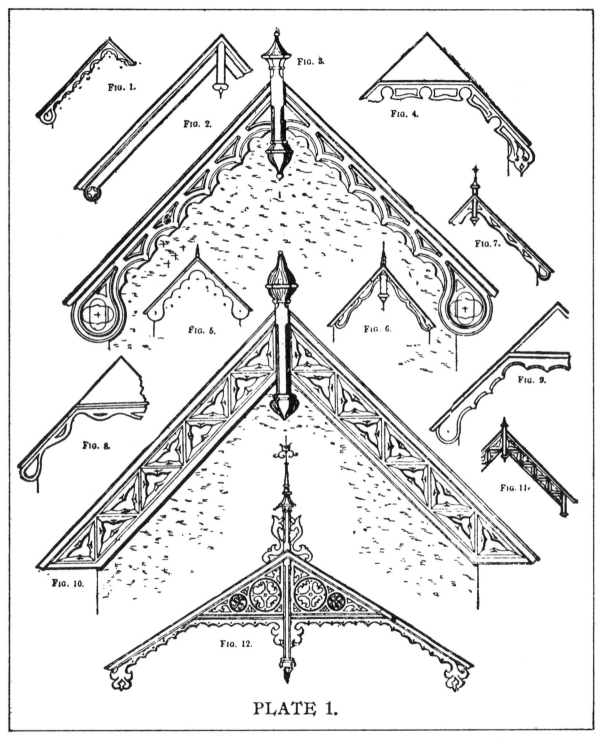

FIG. 1.

FIG. 2.

FIG. 3.

FIG. 4.

FIG. 7.

FIG. 5.

FIG. 6.

FIG. 9.

FIG. 8.

FIG. 11.

FIG. 10.

FIG. 12.

PLATE 1.

ORNAMENTAL BARGEBOARDS   from MODERN CARPENTRY, A PRACTICAL
MANUAL by Fred T. Hodgson, 1902

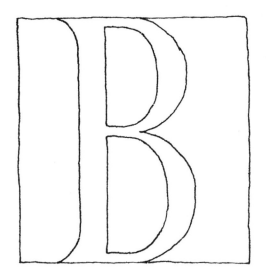

BACKFILL

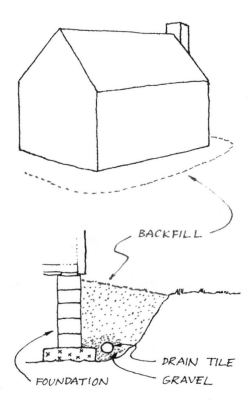

BACKFILL

FOUNDATION

DRAIN TILE

GRAVEL

Backfill is the term commonly given to the gravel and earth that is 'filled back' into the space left around the outside of a foundation, after the foundation has been built in the hole excavated for it.

Backfill should not include scraps of wood or other debris that might attract potentially dangerous insects such as carpenter ants; it should include drain tile; and it should be carefully packed and graded to slope away from the house.

BALUSTER. SEE BANISTER

BALUSTRADE

A balustrade is a row of banisters joined at the top by a handrail serving as a fence for balconies, terraces, and most commonly, staircases

BALUSTRADE

HANDRAIL

BANISTER

BANISTER

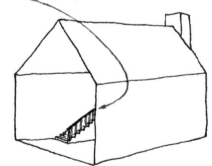

Banister is the now more common form and corruption of baluster, a word which was originally Italian, meaning 'blossom of the wild pomegranate,' the shape of which resembles the short pillars, circular in section, slender above and bulging below, used to support a handrail; banisters and handrail together forming a balustrade. Used in the plural, banisters is the more common term for a staircase balustrade.

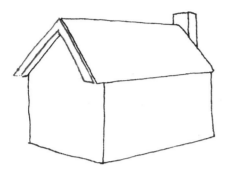

BARGEBOARD
GABLEBOARD
VERGEBOARD

Bargeboards, also called gableboards or vergeboards, are the raking boards found at the gable of a building. Roofs may be constructed in various ways but whenever the framework overhangs the end (gable) walls, a bargeboard is frequently used to cover the projecting ends of the roof timbers. Bargeboards are often the occasion for a variety of ornamentation. The word barge comes from the medieval Latin for gallows — bargeboards originally covered the barge-couple, a pair of strengthening roof beams joined together as are the members of a gallows. (see illustration facing page 19.)

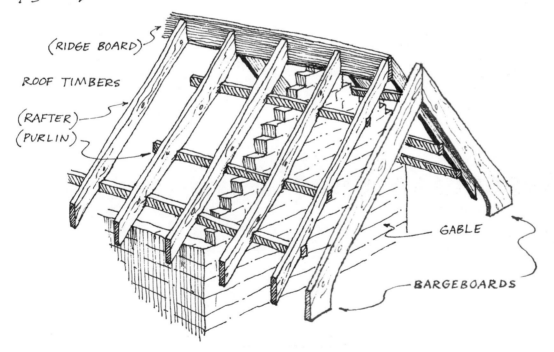

(RIDGE BOARD)

ROOF TIMBERS

(RAFTER)
(PURLIN)

GABLE

BARGEBOARDS

BASEBOARD

The baseboard (known as the skirting or skirtingboard in Britain) is that board, plain or moulded, which runs around the bottom of an interior wall and covers the junction of the floorboards with the wall.

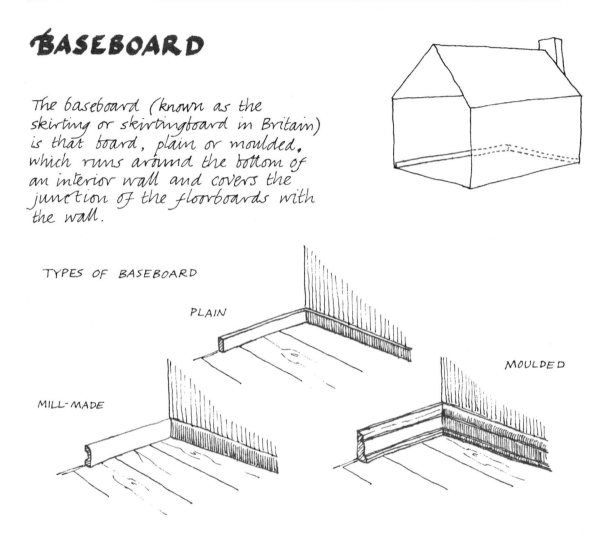

TYPES OF BASEBOARD

PLAIN

MILL-MADE

MOULDED

BASEBOARD SHOE

The baseboard shoe is a thin piece of moulding used to conceal the gap between the bottom of the baseboard and the floor (which may not be perfectly flat).

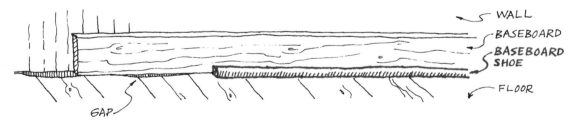

WALL
BASEBOARD
BASEBOARD SHOE
FLOOR
GAP

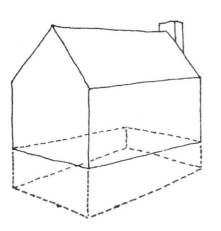

BASEMENT

In Classical architecture basement is that part of the building upon which the columns rest. In Renaissance architecture basement refers to the ground-floor facade. In Modern usage basement refers to the lowest storey of a building when that storey is at least partly below ground or street level.

The distinction between basement and cellar resides in the fact that a cellar is by definition wholly below ground level and intended as a storage area.

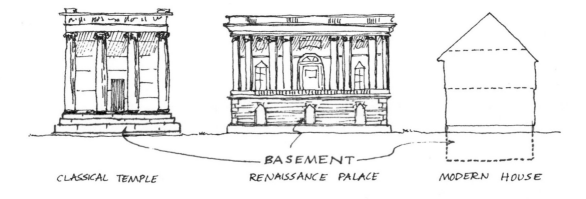

CLASSICAL TEMPLE   — BASEMENT —   MODERN HOUSE
           RENAISSANCE PALACE

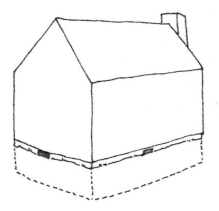

BASEMENT VENT

A basement vent is some kind of ventilation opening, usually screened and sometimes glazed, found in the top of the basement or foundation wall to allow air circulation through an otherwise closed area of the building.

BATTEN

In earlier British usage a batten referred to any piece of wood no larger than "7" broad and 2½" thick (177.8 mm × 63.5 mm), commonly used for such purposes as floorboards. Nowadays, however, when a builder or carpenter says batten he usually means something a bit smaller, such as might be used for bracing together the boards of a board and batten door, or providing a ledge or stiffening piece for several larger boards. Used with wide vertical exterior siding boards, a thin batten covers the gap between adjacent boards (see SIDING, BOARD AND BATTEN).

BAY WINDOW. see WINDOW

BEAM

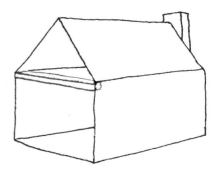

The word beam comes from an older word meaning tree (and still exists in English in the example Hornbeam - a type of tree). While a beam is thus a large squared timber, often made from a whole tree, its use is properly restricted to a timber used horizontally (a vertical timber being called a post). Before the introduction of smaller framing members called studs, all wooden buildings were supported by a framework of variously named beams (and posts); see, for example, COLLAR BEAM, GIRT, SUMMER BEAM, etc. (See illustration facing page 169.)

BEARER

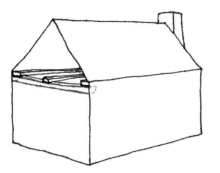

Bearer is used both as a comprehensive term for any supporting part of a house's framework and occasionally as a specific name for a part of a more detailed structure — for example, a staircase bearer is a piece of wood wedged into a masonry wall and which supports the end of a winder (a turning step in a staircase).

BEARING WALL. see WALL

BEDDING

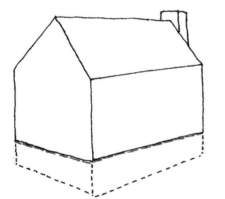

In order to prevent water filling any unevenness between the sill of a house and the top of a foundation wall, the sill is sometimes laid in a bed of (wet) mortar or some other rot-resistant material, such as fiberglass.

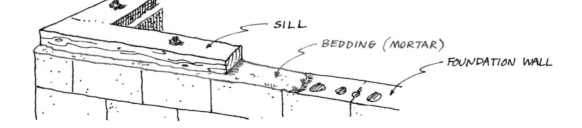

SILL

BEDDING (MORTAR)

FOUNDATION WALL

BED MOULDING

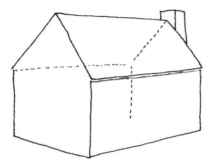

The bed moulding is part of a cornice – an ornamental projection along the top of a building. In small houses the cornice is found where the roof meets the wall.

Classical cornices are made up of many parts, but those found on ordinary residences consist of little more than a few boards covering the bottom ends of the rafters. The bed moulding is used to cover the junction (and any gap) of the soffit and the wall.

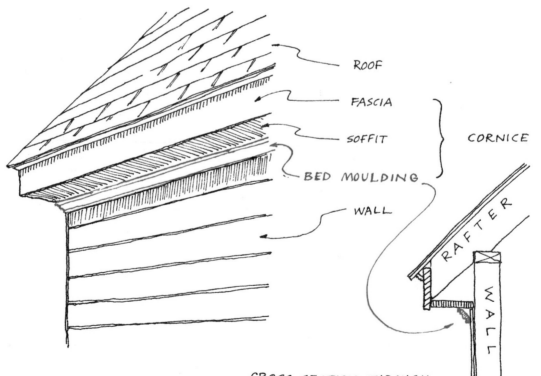

ROOF

FASCIA

SOFFIT ⎫
         ⎬ CORNICE
BED MOULDING ⎭

WALL

RAFTER

WALL

CROSS-SECTION THROUGH RAFTER, CORNICE, & WALL

BEVEL SIDING. see SIDING

BIRDSMOUTH

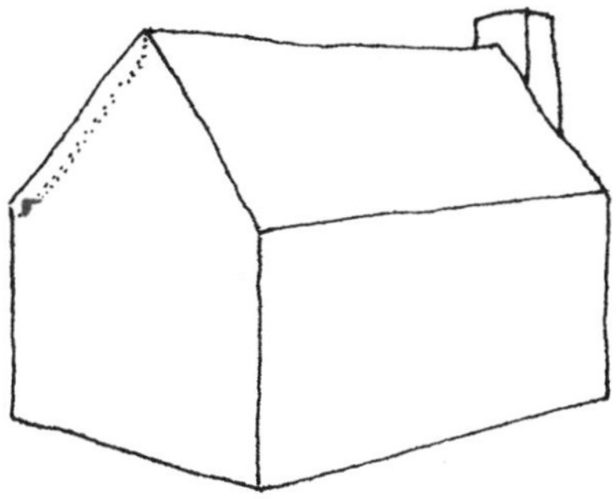

The birdsmouth is an interior angle cut across the grain at the extremity of a timber, typically into the end of a rafter where it rests upon the top plate at the wall.

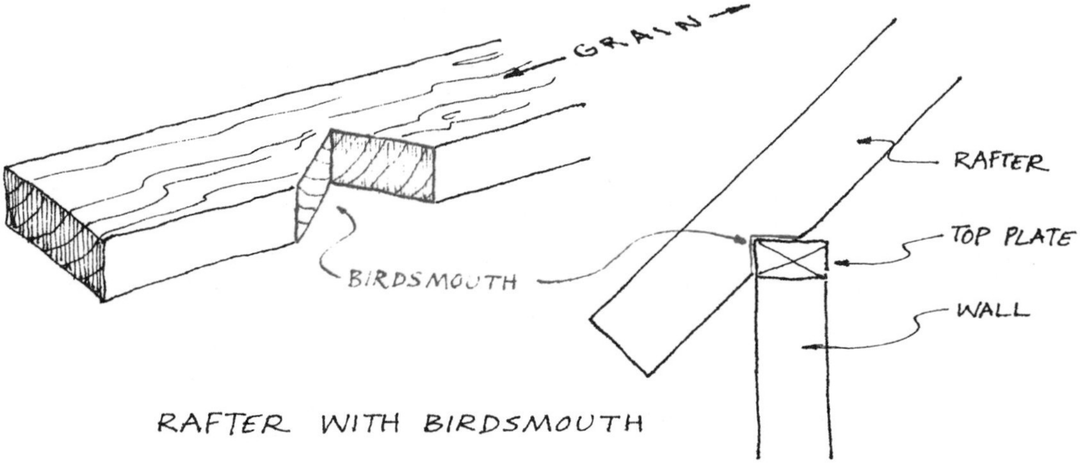

GRAIN

BIRDSMOUTH

RAFTER

TOP PLATE

WALL

RAFTER WITH BIRDSMOUTH

Not all rafters meet the wall upon which they rest at their lower end in the same way, and so not all rafters have birdsmouths.

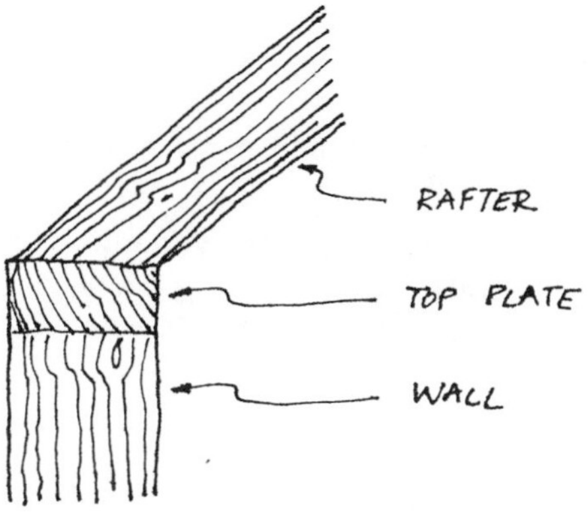

RAFTER

TOP PLATE

WALL

RAFTER WITH NO BIRDSMOUTH

BLOCKING

Blocking consists of pieces of wood the same width as joists, fixed at right angles between the joists to strengthen them and prevent them from bending or twisting. Since it is the joists that support the floor, it is important to ensure a firm framework or the floor will be uncomfortably springy and uneven. A simpler form of blocking is described at BRIDGING.

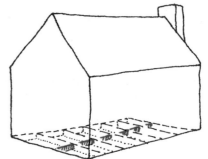

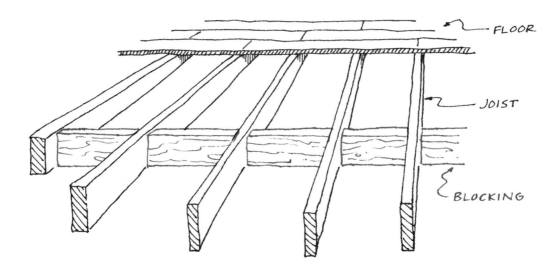

FLOOR

JOIST

BLOCKING

Depending on the size of the joists and the distance spanned between supports and the load the floor is expected to carry, so is the number and location of blocking determined. In a typical small house with 2" × 10" (50.8mm × 254mm) joists, spanning 16' (4.8m), blocking might be installed at the 8' (2.4m) mark.

BOARD AND BATTEN SIDING. see SIDING

BOND

The bond is the pattern in which the bricks are laid up in a brick wall. Different bonds have different properties suited to different purposes. Though there are many variations, most bonds are developments of either the English bond or the Flemish bond.

SOME COMMON BONDS

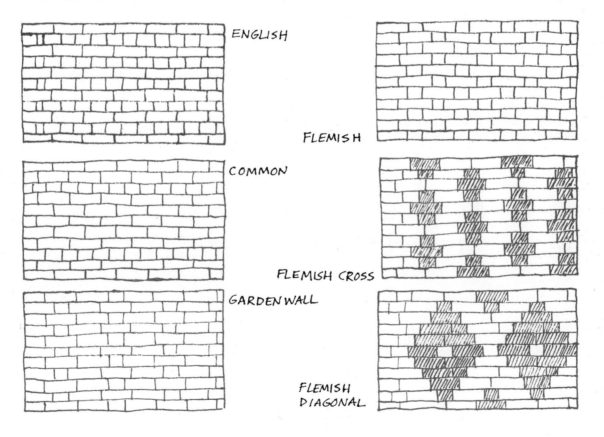

ENGLISH

FLEMISH

COMMON

FLEMISH CROSS

GARDEN WALL

FLEMISH DIAGONAL

BOOT

Boot is the name given to the connecting sleeve between heat registers (grills in the floor or wall through which hot air is forced) and the ductwork which leads to the registers from the furnace.

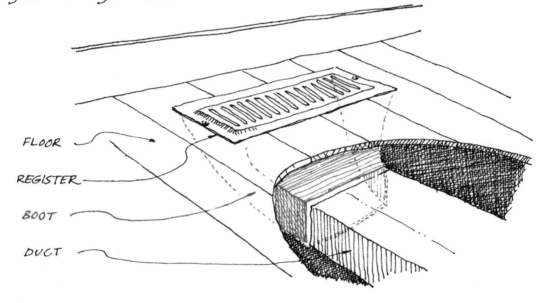

FLOOR

REGISTER

BOOT

DUCT

BOW WINDOW. see WINDOW

BOXINGS

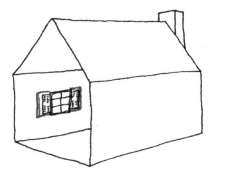

Windows with inside shutters are often built with cases on either side of the window to receive the shutters when they are opened. Such shutters are called boxed shutters, and the casings into which they are folded are known as the boxings.

BRACE

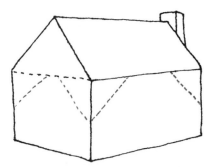

Any diagonally placed timber in a house's framework may constitute a brace, from the heavy timber framing of older buildings to the light stud-constructed buildings common today. The brace's purpose is to impart strength and rigidity.

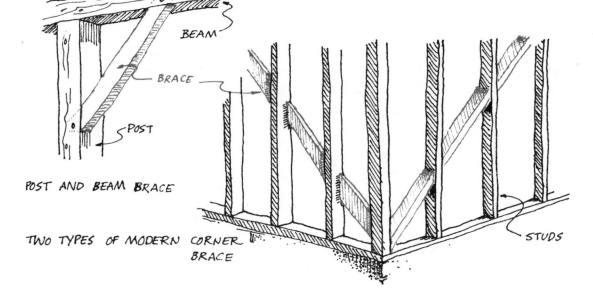

BEAM

BRACE

POST

POST AND BEAM BRACE

TWO TYPES OF MODERN CORNER BRACE

STUDS

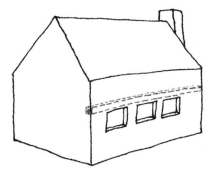

BREASTSUMMER
BRESSUMMER

The word breastsummer (or its common derivative, bressummer) simply means breast beam; summer coming from the French word "sommier" meaning beam. A breast beam is a large horizontal timber used in the breast (face) of a wall, over an opening, supporting the wall above. See also SUMMER BEAM.

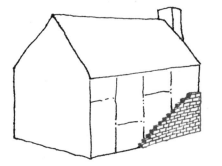

BRICK VENEER

Many houses apparently made of brick are in reality constructed of some other material (with a subsequent outer covering (or veneer) of brick. Brick veneer is used to improve the appearance of concrete-block houses or as an alternative exterior siding material for wood-frame houses which are first sheathed with plywood and then have a single thickness of brick built around them. Brick veneer is much cheaper than a full-bricked house, but can give the same appearance of substantiality.

CONCRETE BLOCK WALL

BRICK VENEER

BRIDGING
CROSS BRIDGING

Bridging may consist of metal straps or small pieces of wood which cross each other diagonally between floor or ceiling joists. A cheaper form of **BLOCKING**, as it uses less wood, bridging is necessary to prevent joists twisting or bending.

FLOOR

JOISTS

CROSS BRIDGING

BUILDING LINES

The building line can mean an imaginary line extended from the corner of a building, or it can refer to one of the various lines when constructing the foundation — such as the **EXCAVATION LINE**, which marks the limit of excavation, or the **FACE LINE**, which marks where the outside of the building will be.

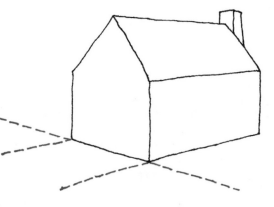

BUILDING PAPER

Building paper, often referred to as felt paper, tar paper, or black paper, is a tar-impregnated feltlike paper used between the various layers of a house (between inside and outside walls, between sub-floors and finish floors, behind paneling, and between roofing boards and roofing shingles) in order to provide a measure of damp-proofing, waterproofing, dust- and wind-proofing. (See illustration facing page 115.)

Another kind of paper, thinner and red in color, called rosin paper, is used for similar reasons but in places where felt paper would be inapplicable, such as under wooden shingles, which must be allowed to 'breathe.'

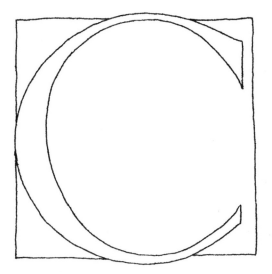

CABINET HEAD

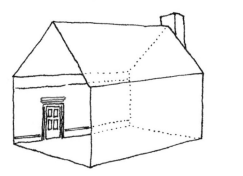

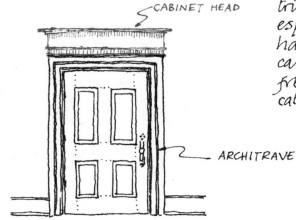

CABINET HEAD

ARCHITRAVE

Cabinet head is the term given to a boxed-in head at the top of an architrave; architrave being a door frame. Many cheap and modern doorways are surrounded by a plain flat trim, but better quality work, especially in older houses, often has an elaborately moulded and carved architrave, which is frequently surmounted by a cabinet head.

CAP COURSE

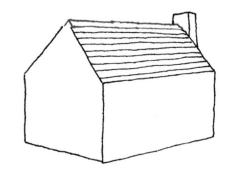

Course is a word much used in building and refers to a layer of something such as bricks or stone, each successive layer being known as a course. A cap course is therefore the topmost course of such an arrangement, but is chiefly used to refer to the topmost course of roof shingles which cap, or cover, the top course of shingles on both sides of the roof where they meet at the ridge.

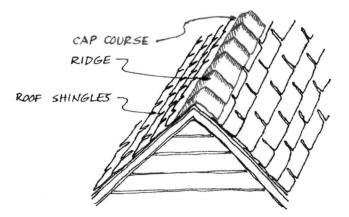

CAP COURSE
RIDGE
ROOF SHINGLES

CARRIAGE

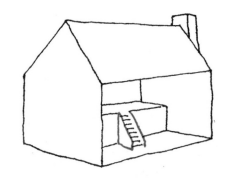

Carriage is the basic framework of a staircase, which includes the side pieces known as stringers which actually 'carry' the steps – properly known as treads. See also STAIRCASE.

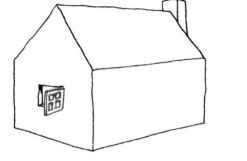

CASEMENT

A casement is a window sash or frame forming a window, which, being hinged to one of the sides of the frame which encloses it, may be opened and closed like a door.

CASEMENT WINDOW. *see* WINDOW

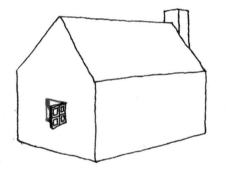

CASING

Casing is a loosely used term which may refer to just the architrave, the trim, or the whole frame in which a door or window is hung. However, the correct meaning of casing is the inner part of the frame in which the door or window is hung, and to which the architrave and other trim details, such as stops, are fixed.

WALL
ARCHITRAVE
STOP

CASING

CORNER OF DOOR FRAME

CAT

A cat is a short piece of wood nailed between studs in a wooden framed-house. The cat is usually made from the same material as the studs, and is commonly 2" x 4" (50mm x 100mm). In good work the cats form a continuous line running horizontally between the studs halfway up (if the wall is high there may be more than one line of cats) where they help stiffen the wall, keep the studs from twisting, and provide an extra nailing surface for subsequent wall coverings.

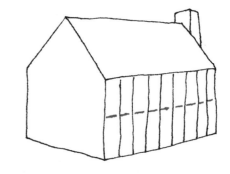

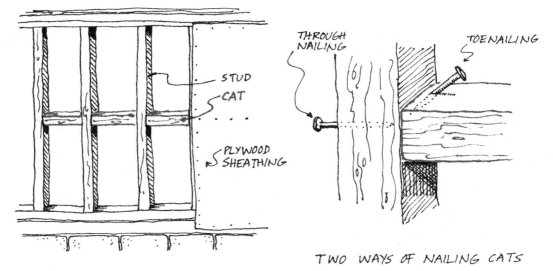

STUD
CAT
PLYWOOD SHEATHING

THROUGH NAILING
TOENAILING

TWO WAYS OF NAILING CATS

CAVITY WALL. see WALL

CEILING

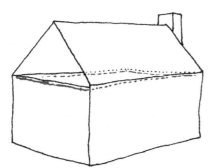

Derived ultimately from the Latin word for sky (cælum), ceiling means properly only the covering (usually of plaster, sometimes of wood or metal) of the roof of a room. A room whose ceiling consists of the uncovered beams and floorboards of the room above cannot strictly be said to have a ceiling, although it must be admitted that in common usage the word ceiling is become synonymous with the roof of a room.

A slightly different ceiling is the drop or suspended ceiling, which consists of a framework holding light tiles or panels suspended some way below the bottom of the floor above.

CELLAR

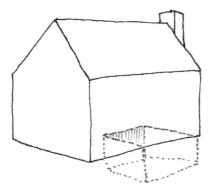

A cellar is an underground store-room, such as a wine cellar or a coal cellar, and is not the same thing as a basement which is not necessarily underground.

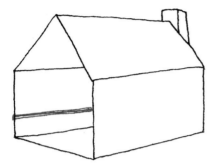

CHAIR RAIL

Older houses were frequently wood-paneled inside. With the rise in popularity of decorated plaster walls the paneling shrank to the bottom half of the room, but reaching at least high enough to protect the plaster walls from damage by various pieces of furniture, especially chairs. Since plaster is cheaper than paneling, it was inevitable that this half-paneling (known as wainscotting) should also disappear leaving behind, however, a wooden moulding at chairback height to protect the wall. This vestige of floor-to-ceiling paneling is known as the chair rail.

PLASTER

CHAIR RAIL

CHASE

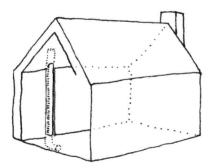

A chase is a groove or space cut or left in a wall to accommodate plumbing or wiring. The plumber is said to chase the pipes through the wall.

CHIMNEY

Although chimney is often taken to mean only that part which rises above the roof, especially in Britain where most chimneys are constructed inside the house, the term actually applies to the whole casing enclosing the flue of a fireplace or furnace through which the smoke ascends to the outside. In Europe most chimneys are finished off with chimney pots - cylindrical earthenware pots at the top of the chimney shaft, but in America the top is either flush or capped with a large stone.

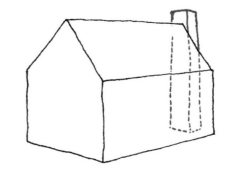

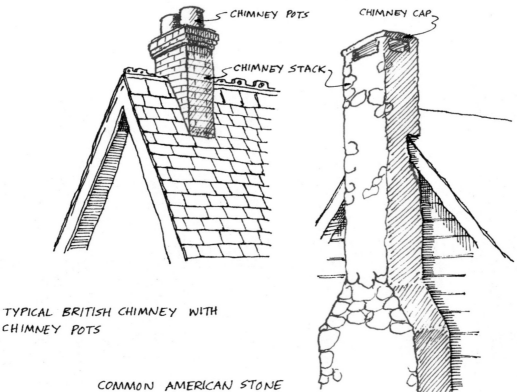

CHIMNEY POTS

CHIMNEY STACK

CHIMNEY CAP

TYPICAL BRITISH CHIMNEY WITH CHIMNEY POTS

COMMON AMERICAN STONE CHIMNEY

CHIMNEY BREAST

A chimney breast is the intrusion into a room by the masonry and its surround of a fireplace and its chimney. Such an interior projection necessarily creates recesses or alcoves on either side which may provide convenient locations for shelves or cupboards.

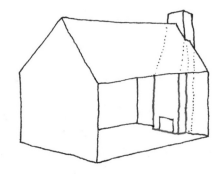

CHIMNEY BREAST

CHIMNEY GIRT. see GIRT

CILL. see SILL

CINDER BLOCK. see CONCRETE BLOCK

CISTERN

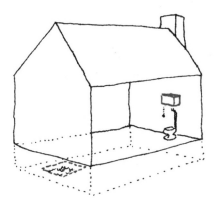

The word cistern comes from the Latin word for box (cista)(as does the word chest) and means a receptacle for the storage of water. Old houses sometimes used cisterns to collect spring and rain water, but a more modern use of the word is to describe the reservoirs of water-closets, especially the separately mounted wooden units of early toilets.

CLADDING. see SIDING

CLAPBOARD(ING). see SIDING

CLOSET

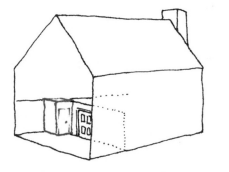

Closet comes from the old French word for little room, and in the Middle Ages this is what it meant. But now the closet has shrunk and is no longer a little room but a rather large cupboard, such as a walk-in wardrobe. There is one exception, however, in the British word for 'rest room' which is similarly euphemistically referred to as a 'water-closet'.

COLLAR BEAM

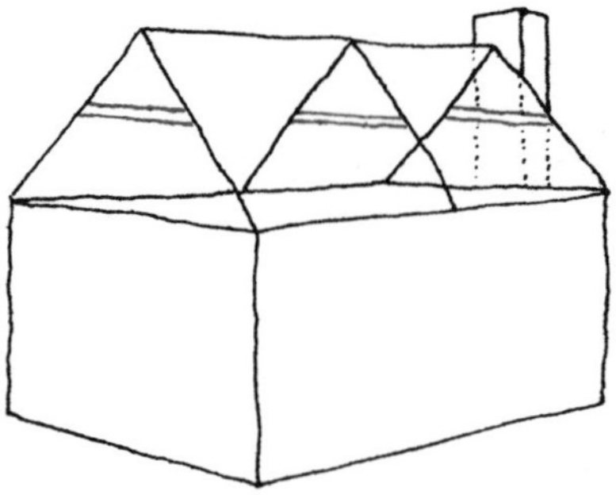

A collar beam is a horizontal member of a roof's framework that connects two opposite rafters somewhere above their lower ends.

A similar beam connected through the lower ends of rafters is known as a tie beam, and it may be said that the collar beam is a sort of tie beam.

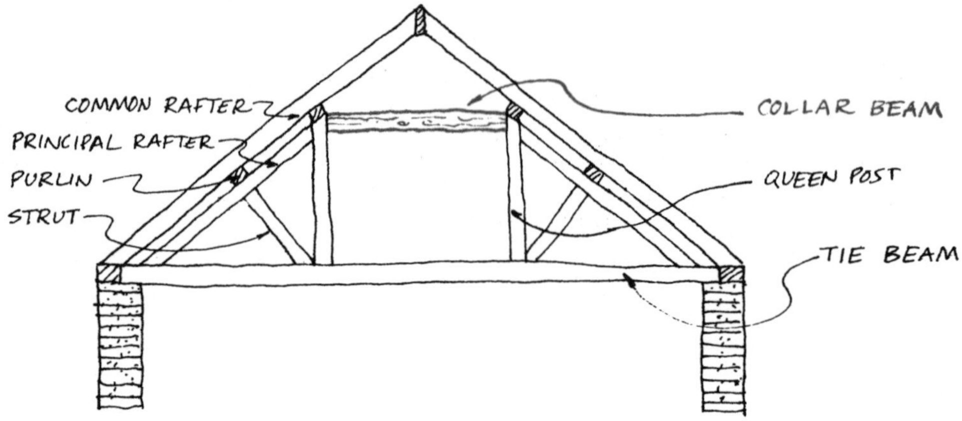

COMMON RAFTER

PRINCIPAL RAFTER

PURLIN

STRUT

COLLAR BEAM

QUEEN POST

TIE BEAM

TWO TYPES OF ROOF USING COLLAR BEAMS

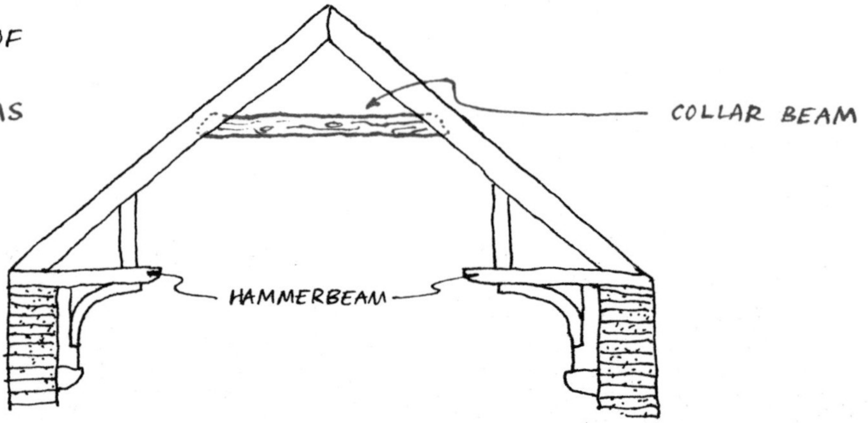

COLLAR BEAM

HAMMERBEAM

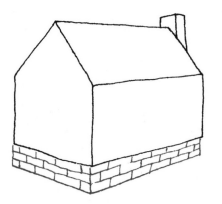

CONCRETE BLOCK
CEMENT BLOCK
CINDER BLOCK

A hollow rectangular unit made of portland cement concrete, with a coarse aggregate of well-burned coal cinders, is what is commonly known as a concrete block. Made in various shapes and sizes, the concrete block is a part of most American houses today, used in piers, foundations, chimneys, and sometimes in the construction of entire houses.

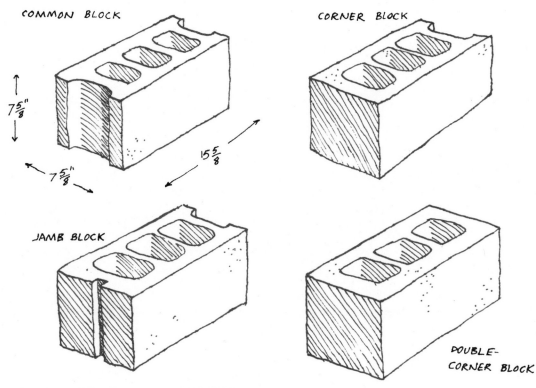

COMMON BLOCK

CORNER BLOCK

$7\frac{5}{8}$"

$7\frac{5}{8}$"

$15\frac{5}{8}$

JAMB BLOCK

DOUBLE-CORNER BLOCK

VARIOUS BLOCK SHAPES

CONDUCTOR. see DOWNSPOUT

COPING

Coping is the name given to the topmost course (layer) of a wall. The coping is usually made of sloping stone or tile in order to throw off water and protect the wall.

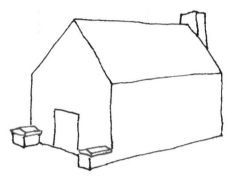

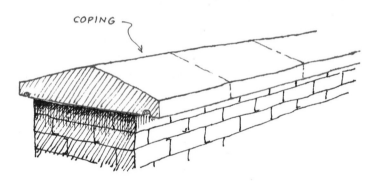

COPING

CORBEL

A corbel (from the Latin word for raven) is a projecting part of a wall so built in order to provide a better support for any superincumbent weight. Eaves which project in order to accommodate an overhanging roof are known as corbeled eaves.

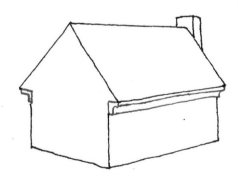

CORNER BEAD

Used mainly with interior plaster and sheetrock walls, corner beads are angled metal strips which protect exposed corners from chipping and denting.

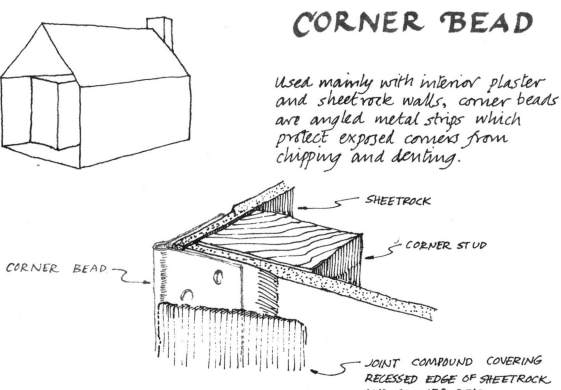

SHEETROCK

CORNER STUD

CORNER BEAD

JOINT COMPOUND COVERING RECESSED EDGE OF SHEETROCK AND CORNER BEAD

CORNER BOARD

Corner boards are used to trim the corners of wooden-sided houses and protect the ends of the horizontal siding.

THREE WAYS OF FIXING CORNER BOARDS

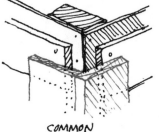 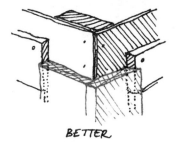 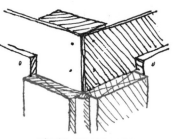

COMMON   BETTER   MOST ELEGANT

47

CORNER BRACE. *see* BRACE

CORNICE

Although in classical architecture cornice refers to the highest part of an entablature resting on the frieze, in the common house the cornice is the boxed-in area at the top of a wall upon which the rafters rest.

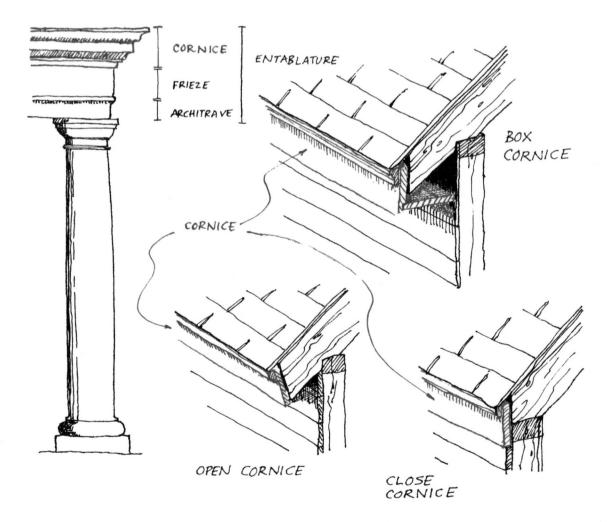

CORNICE

FRIEZE

ARCHITRAVE

ENTABLATURE

BOX CORNICE

CORNICE

OPEN CORNICE

CLOSE CORNICE

CORNICE RETURN

Older wooden buildings often carried the cornice (see previous page) around the gable end of a building for a little way, and this section of cornice is known as the cornice return. (A cornice which continues all the way across this end of the building is known as a rake cornice.)

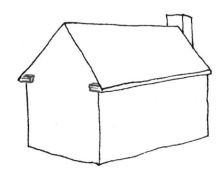

GABLE END

ROOF

CORNICE

CORNICE RETURN

COURSE

A course is a horizontal row of bricks, blocks, stone, or other masonry material that 'runs' around the building. Course is also applied to rows of roof shingles.

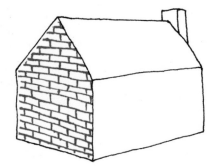

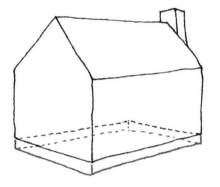

CRAWL SPACE

A house with no basement, unless it is built directly on solid rock or on a poured concrete slab, will usually have a space large enough to crawl through beneath the floor. This crawl space, generally unfinished, is used for visual inspection of pipes and ducts.

CREEPER . see TAIL

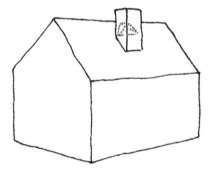

CRICKET

Where a chimney rises through a sloping roof, provision must be made to prevent water collecting behind the chimney. The cricket is a small structure designed to lead water away from such a chimney.

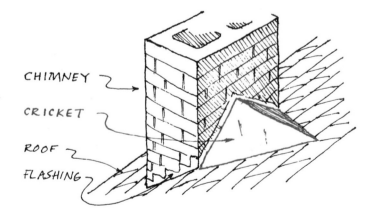

CHIMNEY

CRICKET

ROOF

FLASHING

CRIPPLE

A cripple stud or rafter is one of a series of such framing members, which being intercepted by another framing member, is shorter than the rest of the series. A distinction is sometimes made between a cripple (stud or rafter) and a jack (stud or rafter): the cripple is shorter at its foot, whereas the jack is shorter in its height; however, the two terms are often used synonymously

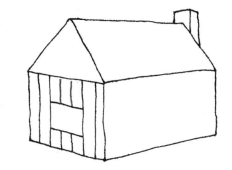

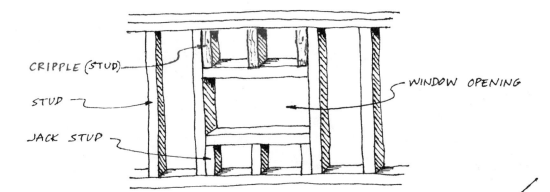

CRIPPLE (STUD)

STUD

JACK STUD

WINDOW OPENING

SECTION OF WALL FRAMING

A cripple is also the name given to spars set up as shores against the sides of buildings

CRIPPLE

CROSS BRIDGING. see BRIDGING

CROWN MOULDING

A crown moulding is a particularly large-sectioned moulding, formerly cut by hand with large crown moulding planes, but now available at most lumberyards in mill-made lengths. Crown mouldings are typically used in high corners, such as at the top of a room or along the top of a cornice.

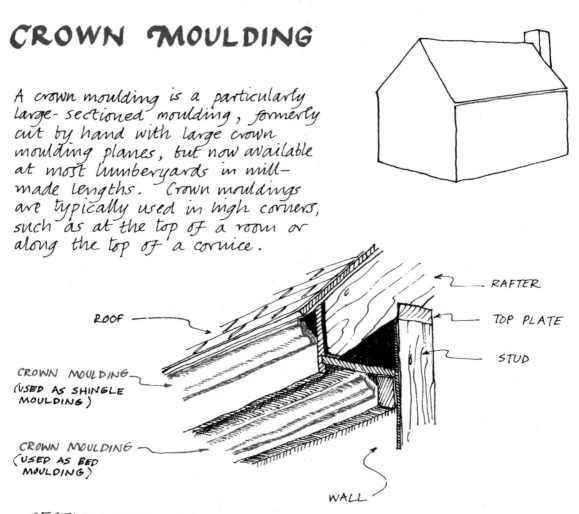

ROOF

CROWN MOULDING
(USED AS SHINGLE MOULDING)

CROWN MOULDING
(USED AS BED MOULDING)

RAFTER

TOP PLATE

STUD

WALL

SECTION THROUGH CORNICE

CUPBOARD

Originally a simple board or table on which cups and plates were kept, the cupboard has grown over the centuries to become a small closet, generally fitted with shelves, in which all manner of things may be kept.

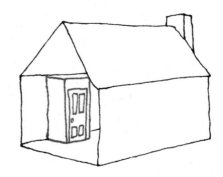

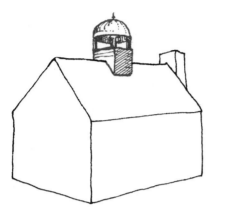

CUPOLA

Originally a small dome on the top of a roof, a cupola (from the Latin for little barrel, and from which Latin origin we get our word for cup) is now used to indicate any small structure built on the top of a roof to provide a lookout, interior lighting, or simply ornamentation.

CURTAIN WALL. see PARTITION

5 3

PLATE XXXVII

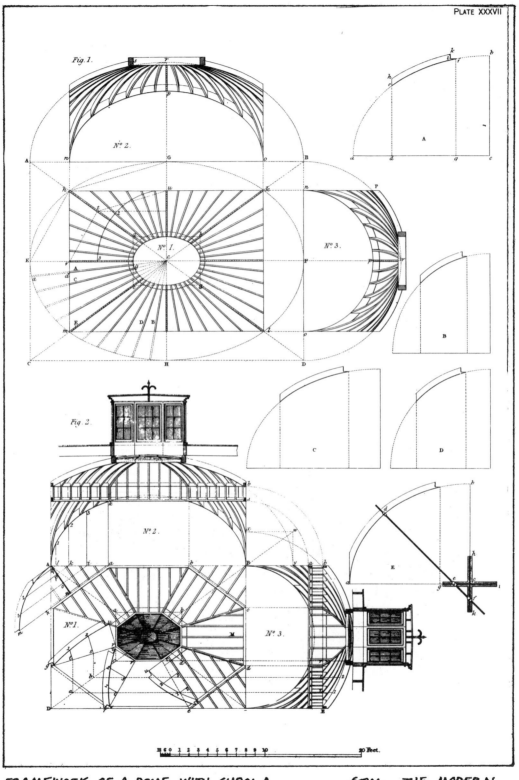

FRAMEWORK OF A DOME WITH CUPOLA   from THE MODERN
CARPENTER JOINER AND CABINET-MAKER   by G. LISTER SUTCLIFFE, 1903

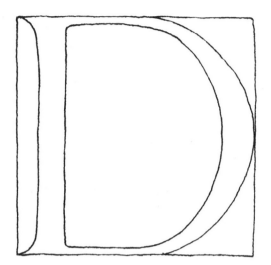

DADO

The word dado has two meanings nowadays; one describes a kind of woodworking joint, the other describes any wall covering that covers only the lower part of a wall — typically a half-paneled wall. The word comes from the Italian for die — meaning not death, but that portion of a pedestal between the base and the cornice. Since wood paneling often resembles a pedestal, dado was used to describe first the central part, later the entire paneling, and ultimately any lower wall covering at all.

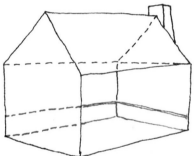

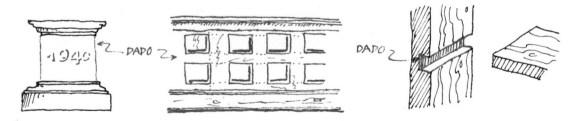

DAMPCOURSE

Houses constructed of brick, especially in Britain where it is required by law, often have a layer of some waterproof material built into the wall at the top and bottom. This is known as the dampcourse.

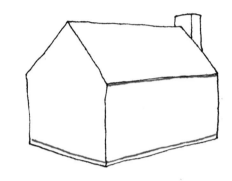

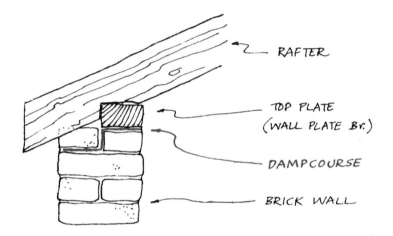

RAFTER

TOP PLATE
(WALL PLATE Br.)

DAMPCOURSE

BRICK WALL

DECK

A deck is a frequently found part of country houses, and consists of an attached platform often built out from the house where the ground slopes steeply away.

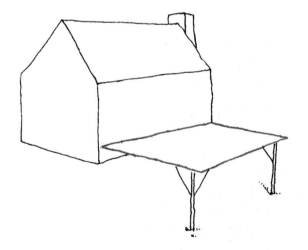

DIAGONAL SHEATHING. see SHEATHING

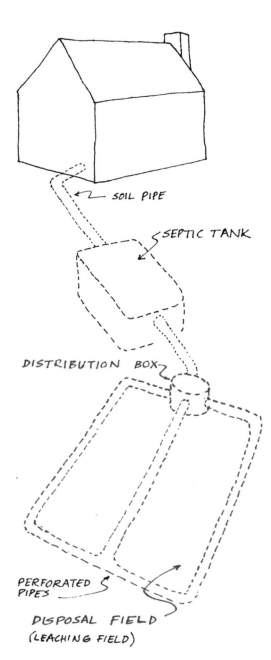

SOIL PIPE

SEPTIC TANK

DISTRIBUTION BOX

PERFORATED
PIPES

DISPOSAL FIELD
(LEACHING FIELD)

DISPOSAL FIELD

The disposal field is that part of a house's sewage system where the sewage liquid, after having separated from the solid sewage in the septic tank, is leaked into the surrounding ground to be completely decomposed by bacteria.

To be effective the septic tank must be in order and the surrounding ground properly prepared in order to be capable of sufficient drainage. For houses built close together a central sewage system is more usual, although there are now more modern systems than the septic tank, such as composting toilets.

DISTRIBUTION BOX

The distribution box is a small tank that distributes the liquid from the septic tank to the various perforated pipes of the disposal field.

DOOR

A door is a movable barrier which seals the access to a house or a room or other space within a house.

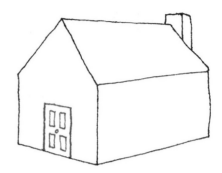

Doors may be classified by purpose — for example, entrance door, front door, back door, kitchen door, interior door, exterior door, garage door, cupboard door, etc.; or by their construction — for example, dutch door, flush door, glass door, sliding door, revolving door, etc. (See page 108.)

For many centuries the best-constructed doors have been wooden panel doors. The construction of the frame provides a large surface resistant to warping, and the panels provide a means of accommodating the inevitable shrinking and swelling of wood without damage to the door.

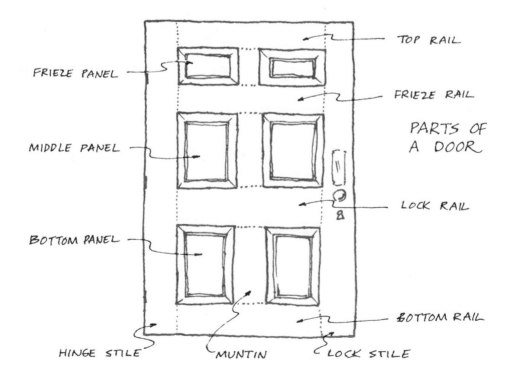

PARTS OF A DOOR

- TOP RAIL
- FRIEZE PANEL
- FRIEZE RAIL
- MIDDLE PANEL
- LOCK RAIL
- BOTTOM PANEL
- BOTTOM RAIL
- HINGE STILE
- MUNTIN
- LOCK STILE

DOOR BUCK

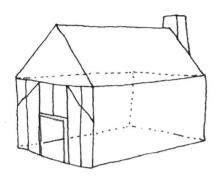

Door buck is the name given to the rough opening left for a door in the framing of a wood house. Door buck can also refer to the rough frame in which the finished door frame will eventually be built.

DOOR BUTT. see HINGE

DOOR FRAME

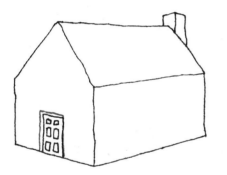

The door frame is that part of the surrounding woodwork of a door to which the door is actually hinged, although in loose usage sometimes the whole architrave, casing, and trim is meant.

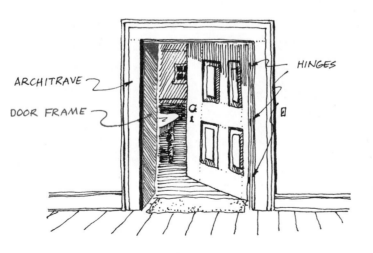

ARCHITRAVE

DOOR FRAME

HINGES

DORMER

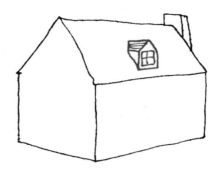

Dormer comes from dormitory which means sleeping place. Since attic rooms (rooms built in the roof) were often used as sleeping places, the vertical casements set in the sloping roof to hold windows to light this area became known as dormers; the windows themselves properly being known as dormer windows. (Windows set flush in a roof are known as skylights.) (See illustrations facing pages **67** and **123**.)

DOUBLE HEADER

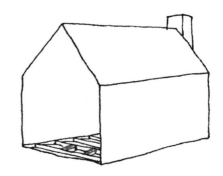

A header is a joist placed at right angles to the regular joists, usually covering and connecting the 'heads' or ends of the joists. A double header is used to frame out an opening left in the floor between joists, for a trapdoor or stairwell.

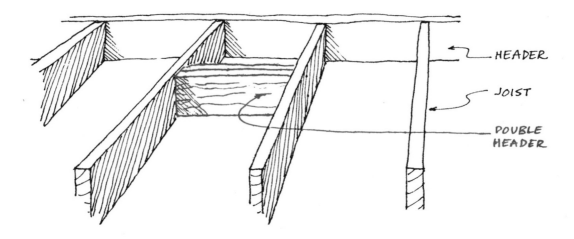

HEADER

JOIST

DOUBLE HEADER

DOUBLE-HUNG WINDOW. see WINDOW

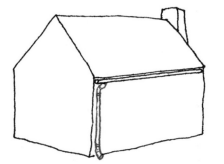

DOWNSPOUT
CONDUCTOR
LEADER

The downspout (conductor or leader) is the pipe which leads the water collected in the gutters of a house to the ground. Without gutters and downspouts to drain them, rain from the roof might quickly erode a trench around the house and damage the siding. The downspout leads the water to a drain or a cistern for storage.

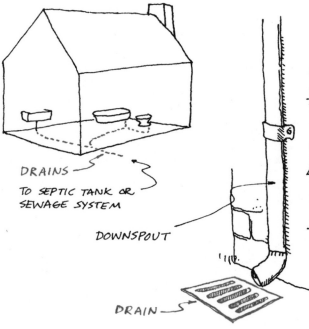

DRAINS

TO SEPTIC TANK OR
SEWAGE SYSTEM

DOWNSPOUT

DRAIN

DRAIN

Drain can refer to the grating through which water runs into a drainage system below (as at the foot of a downspout), or used in the plural it can refer to all the pipes in a house which carry away the waste water from bathrooms, toilets and sinks.

DRAINAGE TILE

Two different products may be meant by the term drainage tile, although they both have to do with drainage. One, the clay drainage tile, is designed to drain water from the surrounding ground and lead it away, thus draining the ground. The other, a bituminous perforated pipe, although it is often used for the same purpose, especially around the bottom of foundations, is also used to disperse water, as in the disposal field of a sewage system (see DISPOSAL FIELD).

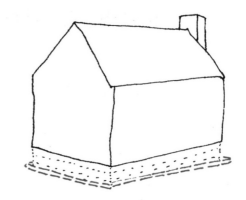

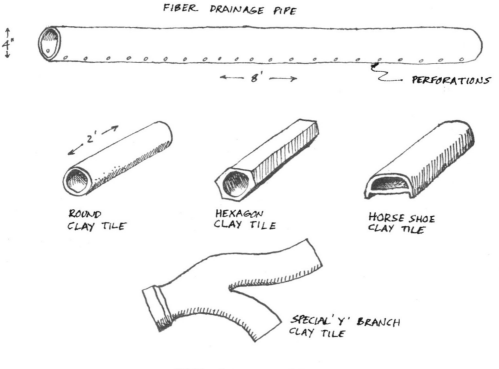

FIBER DRAINAGE PIPE

4"

8'

PERFORATIONS

ROUND CLAY TILE   2'

HEXAGON CLAY TILE

HORSE SHOE CLAY TILE

SPECIAL 'Y' BRANCH CLAY TILE

DRAINAGE TILES

DRIP CAP

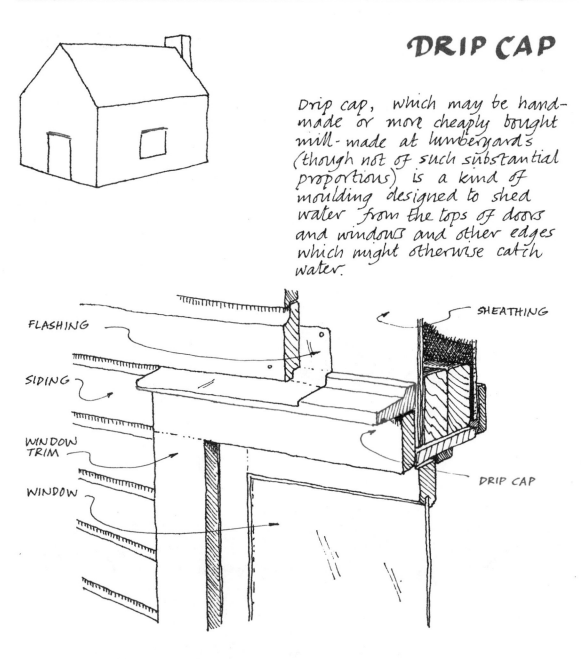

Drip cap, which may be hand-made or more cheaply bought mill-made at lumberyards (though not of such substantial proportions) is a kind of moulding designed to shed water from the tops of doors and windows and other edges which might otherwise catch water.

FLASHING

SHEATHING

SIDING

WINDOW TRIM

WINDOW

DRIP CAP

CROSS-SECTION THROUGH TOP OF
WINDOW SHOWING DRIP CAP ~

DRIP EDGE

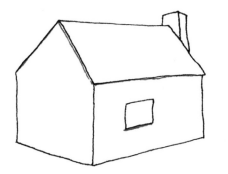

1. Metal drip edge is a section of galvanized metal which is fixed around the edge of the roof to protect the edges of the roof boards or sheathing, secure the edges of the roofing felt, and prevent rain from running down the fascia.

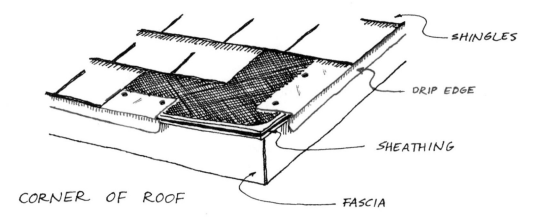

SHINGLES

DRIP EDGE

SHEATHING

CORNER OF ROOF

FASCIA

2. Wooden drip edge may be formed by grooving the outer underside of a board exposed to the weather. The groove thus formed causes any water running down the face of the board to drip off and not run underneath and behind the board below.

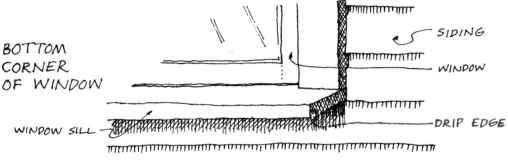

BOTTOM
CORNER
OF WINDOW

SIDING

WINDOW

DRIP EDGE

WINDOW SILL

DROP

A drop is the bottom part of a newel which does not end in a floor but which hangs down into the room or area below. (A newel is the post to which hand-rails for stairs are attached.)

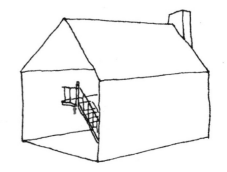

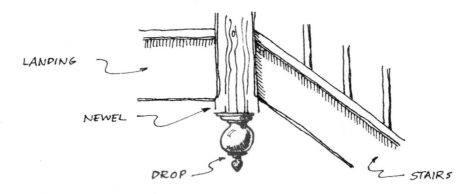

LANDING

NEWEL

DROP

STAIRS

DROP SIDING. see SIDING

DRYWALL. see SHEETROCK

DUCT

A duct is any enclosed channel, normally hidden above the ceiling, behind the walls, or under the floor for the passage of wiring or hot or cold air (see BOOT).

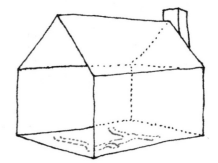

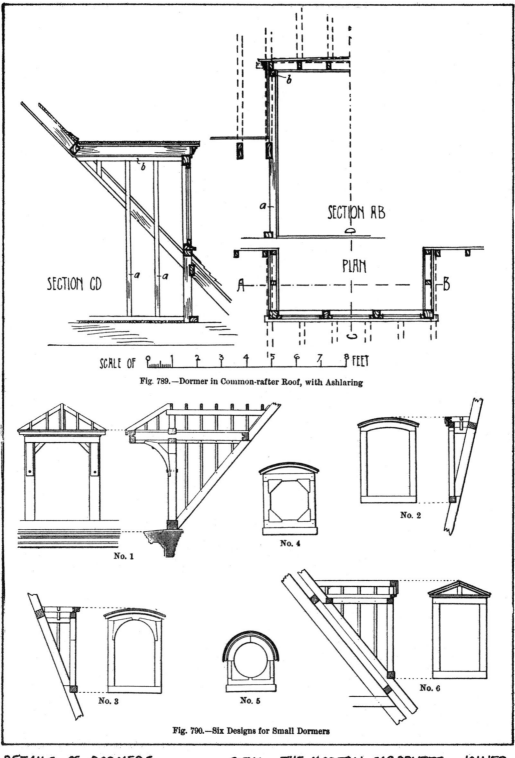

SECTION CD

SECTION AB

PLAN

A   B

C

SCALE OF 1 2 3 4 5 6 7 8 FEET

Fig. 789.—Dormer in Common-rafter Roof, with Ashlaring

No. 1

No. 2

No. 3

No. 4

No. 5

No. 6

Fig. 790.—Six Designs for Small Dormers

DETAILS OF DORMERS   from THE MODERN CARPENTER JOINER
AND CABINET-MAKER by G. LISTER SUTCLIFFE, 1903

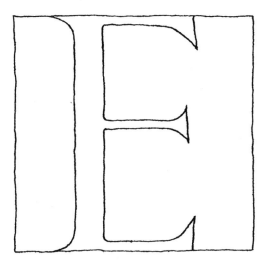

EAVE

The word eave is used as the supposed singular of the word eaves, which because of its terminal 's' is thought to be plural. However, this is not the case. Eaves, which refers to that part of the roof which hangs over the face of the wall which supports it, comes originally from the old word 'efes' which simply meant over, and is really singular.

Strictly speaking, the eaves may continue around all sides of the house, but it has become common to refer to the eaves at the gable end of a house as the rake. Rake actually refers to the slope of the roof, but it is a useful distinction in roof building to divide the eaves into eaves and rake.

EAVE VENT

Modern houses are now almost always built with much insulation. Those which use fiberglass insulation between the rafters must provide some means of ventilation for the space between the insulation and the underside of the roof itself or there will ultimately be damage to the wood from condensation. Eave vents may take several forms, but all provide for the passage of air into this space from the eaves.

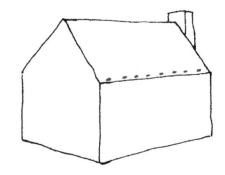

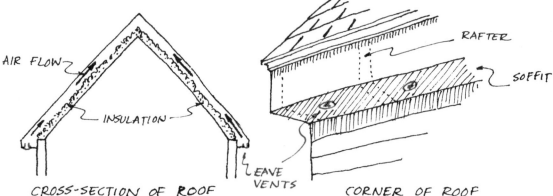

CROSS-SECTION OF ROOF
SHOWING EAVE VENTS AND
AIR FLOW BETWEEN ROOF
AND INSULATION

CORNER OF ROOF
SHOWING EAVE VENTS
IN SOFFIT, BETWEEN
RAFTERS

ELECTRICAL WIRING

Electrical wiring is like the veins and arteries of a house. The wiring and all its accessories run virtually everywhere in the house, just below the surface, supplying electricity wherever it is needed.

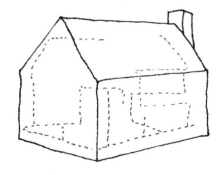

END GIRT. see GIRT

EXCAVATION LINE

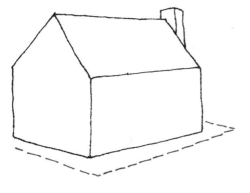

After a building site has been cleared of trees and brush, the first job is to mark on the ground (often with garden lime since this shows up well) exactly where the bulldozer must excavate. This area of excavation is necessarily larger than the intended building since it must include not only the foundation, but room to work on it, and space for exterior foundation drainage.

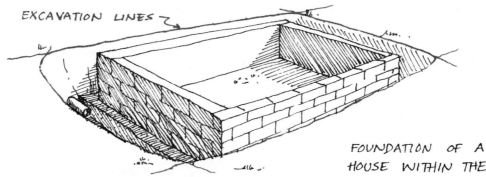

EXCAVATION LINES

FOUNDATION OF A HOUSE WITHIN THE EXCAVATION

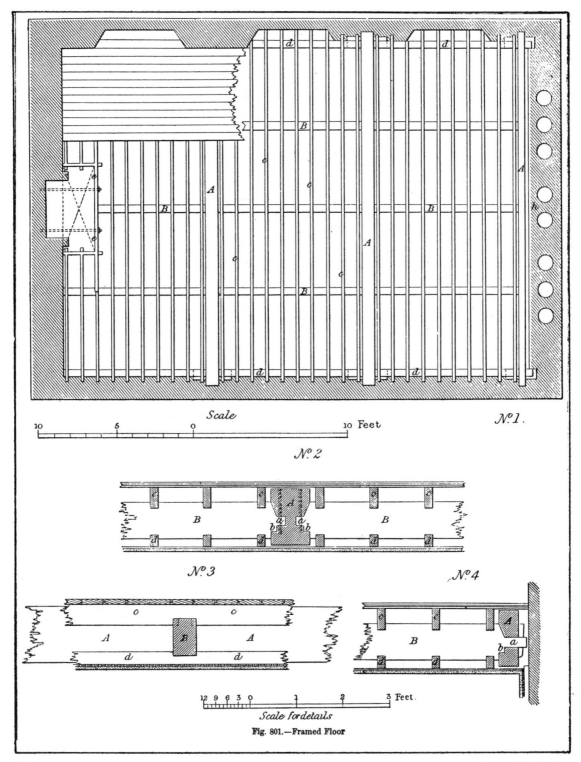

Scale

10   5   0   10 Feet

N°.1.

N°.2

N°.3   N°.4

12 9 6 3 0   1   2   3 Feet.

Scale for details

Fig. 801.—Framed Floor

WOODEN FLOOR   from THE MODERN CARPENTER JOINER AND CABINET-MAKER by G. LISTER SUTCLIFFE, 1903

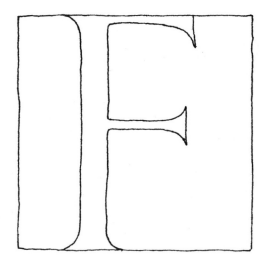

FACE LINE

The face line is the line (usually of string) erected on a building site to mark the exact location of the outside of the foundation and thereby provide a guide to the masons when they are building these walls. Face lines must be made extremely accurate, and are usually stretched between batter boards.

FACE LINE

FUTURE FOUNDATION

BATTER BOARDS

FANLIGHT

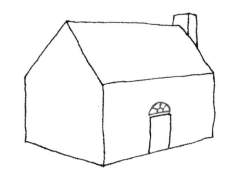

Although any window over a
door may now be referred to
as a fanlight, originally the
term was reserved for fan-
shaped windows (referred to as
lights by architects and builders)
such as were common over
Georgian entrance doors, where
light was admitted to the entrance hall without any
sacrifice of privacy – although subsequently sidelights were
often used as well.

FASCIA

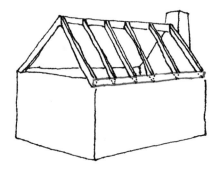

A fascia is any broad flat
surface, such as a band around
a house, but more usually meant
is the board which covers the
ends of the rafters.

FELT PAPER . *see* BUILDING PAPER

FILLER BLOCK

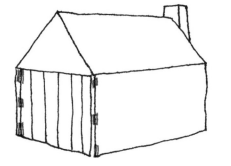

A *filler block* is a short length of wood used to block out the two spaced studs in a three-stud corner post, in a wood-framed building. The filler block keeps these two studs parallel and also provides a little extra nailing surface.

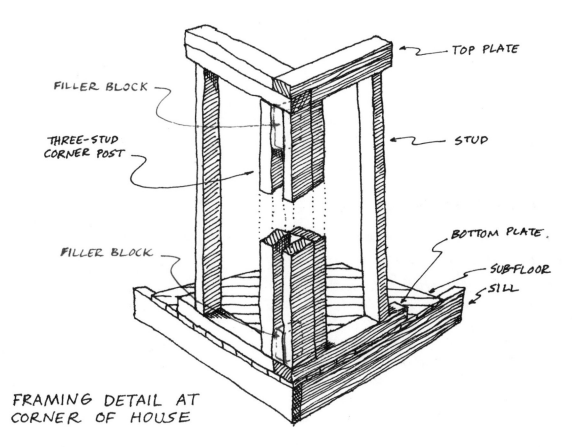

TOP PLATE

FILLER BLOCK

THREE-STUD CORNER POST

STUD

FILLER BLOCK

BOTTOM PLATE.

SUBFLOOR

SILL

FRAMING DETAIL AT CORNER OF HOUSE

FINIAL

A finial is a formal ornament at the top of something, be it the back of a chair, the top of a newel post, or the peak of a roof. (See illustration facing page 19.)

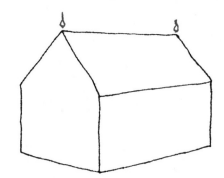

GABLE FINIAL FROM
A VICTORIAN ROOF

FINISH FLOOR

All but the cheapest structures are constructed with two floors, the sub-floor, which is laid directly over the floor joists, and the finish floor which is then laid in a different direction over the subfloor. Two-floor construction provides strength and dust and airtightness.

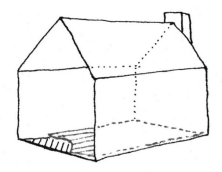

FIREBOX

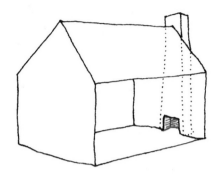

The firebox is that part of a fireplace where the fire actually burns and which is consequently lined with special firebrick — forming, as it were, an additional box within the fireplace.

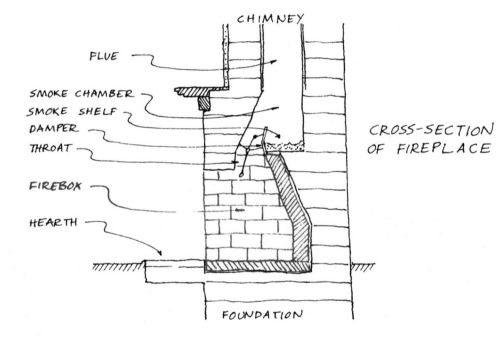

CHIMNEY

FLUE

SMOKE CHAMBER
SMOKE SHELF
DAMPER
THROAT

FIREBOX

HEARTH

CROSS-SECTION
OF FIREPLACE

FOUNDATION

FIREPLACE

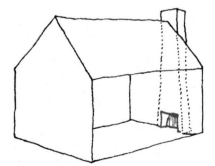

The fireplace is the whole lower part of a chimney, which includes the hearth, the firebox, the throat, the damper, the smoke shelf and the smoke chamber.

FIXED WINDOW. see WINDOW

FIXTURES

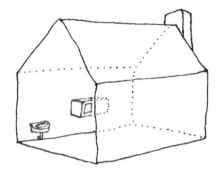

The term *fixtures* in relation to a house refers to things which while not an integral part of the building's structure are nonetheless relatively permanently installed. There are plumbing fixtures, such as sinks, tubs, and toilets; electrical fixtures such as lights, lamps, and water heaters; and heating fixtures such as furnaces, among others. Built-in woodwork, such as counters and cabinets, may also be considered fixtures.

FLASHING

Flashing consists of strips of copper or aluminum so placed as to prevent leaks in corners, and around chimneys (see CRICKET), windows (see DRIP CAP), and doors.

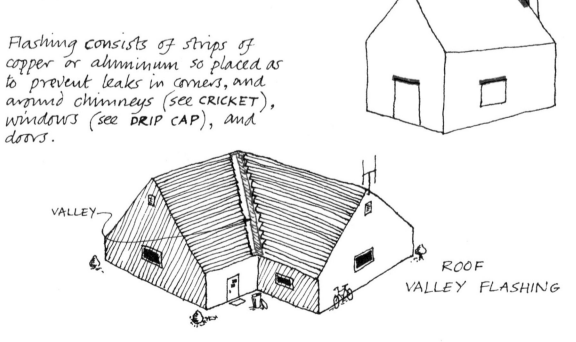

VALLEY

ROOF
VALLEY FLASHING

FLIER

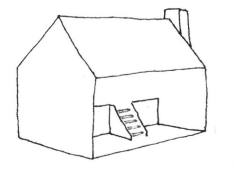

As there are differently shaped staircases so are there different treads - the parts one actually steps upon. Fliers are the simplest kind, found in a straight flight of stairs, and are, by definition, straight, parallel-sided steps. (See also WINDER.)

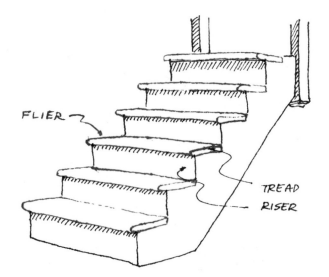

FLIER

TREAD
RISER

FLOOR

The floor is that part of the house on which one walks, and may range from a packed-dirt floor to an elaborate parquet floor. Usually made of hardwood, such as oak or maple for long wear; floors of pine are also common. (see illustration facing page 71.)

FLOOR BOARD

Floor boards are the individual pieces of wood which constitute a finish floor. Floor boards may be made from various kinds of wood and may be made in a large variety of sizes, although today smaller boards are more common.

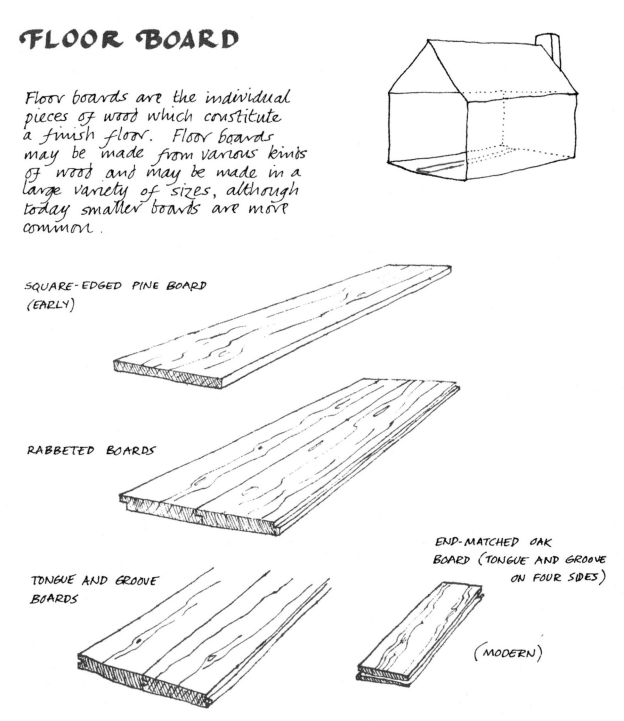

SQUARE-EDGED PINE BOARD
(EARLY)

RABBETED BOARDS

TONGUE AND GROOVE
BOARDS

END-MATCHED OAK
BOARD (TONGUE AND GROOVE
ON FOUR SIDES)

(MODERN)

VARIOUS FLOOR BOARDS

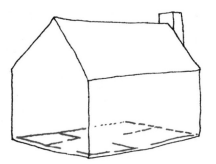

FLOOR PLAN

A floor plan is one of the blue-prints drawn up of a proposed house and is designed to show the exact location of the various rooms, doors, windows, and stairs, etc. Together with a foundation plan and various elevations, the floor plan shows the builder what to build and where, but more importantly it is usually the floor plan which receives most consideration from the prospective home owner, who wants to know how the house will be laid out.

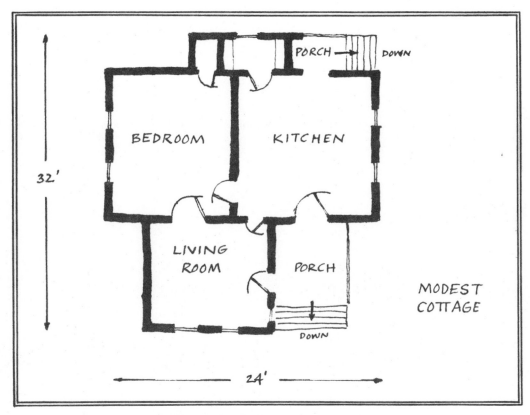

A VICTORIAN FLOOR PLAN, 1890

FLUE

The flue is the enclosed passageway in a chimney, which conveys the smoke, gas, and fumes from a fire to the outside. The construction of a correctly proportioned flue is critical to the proper functioning of a fireplace.

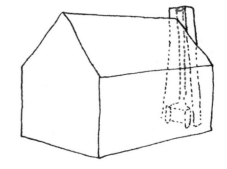

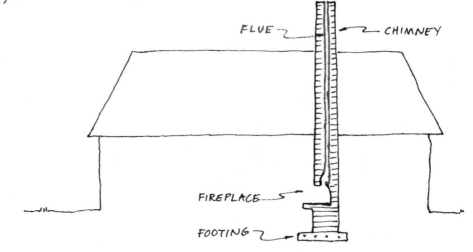

FOOTING

A footing is a concrete base which supports masonry, such as a foundation wall, a pier, or a fireplace and chimney (see FLUE).

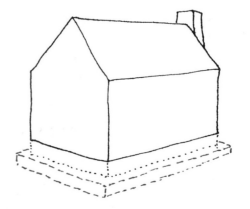

FOUNDATION

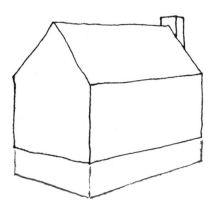

Technically, the foundation is that part of a building which meets the ground, and through which all loads are transferred to the ground.

In the common house the foundation usually consists of concrete block walls, or reinforced concrete walls, built upon a footing or concrete slab. When these walls enclose a space large enough to walk around in, this is known as a full foundation. Older houses used stone (dry-laid (without mortar) or cemented) or brick.

Sometimes the foundation for a house takes the form of piers — which are columns of wood, stone, metal, or concrete, which support the house like so many legs.

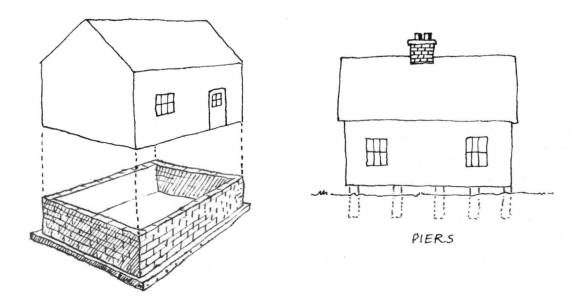

FULL FOUNDATION

PIERS

FOUNDATION COATING

In order to help waterproof
foundation walls they are
sometimes given a covering of
foundation coating. This is a
bituminous substance, painted
onto the outside of the
foundation walls like tar.

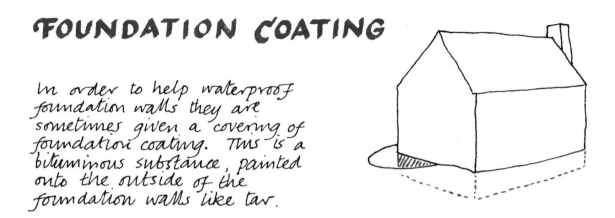

FOUNDATION
COATING

FOUNDATION OFFERING

In order to propitiate certain
gods for breaking the ground,
and in order to ensure the
future stability and endurance
of a building, it was once the
custom to bury live virgins in the
foundation. Such drastic measures
are no longer resorted to, but a
vestige thereof is seen in some
builders' habit of throwing a few
coins into a new foundation as a token offering.

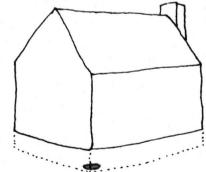

FOUNDATION VENT

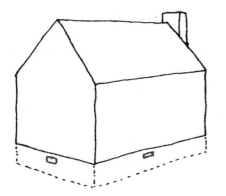

In order to provide ventilation to a basement or crawl space, a series of foundation vents are usually incorporated in the top of a foundation wall. These vents commonly consist of screened grills which may be slid open or closed according to the season.

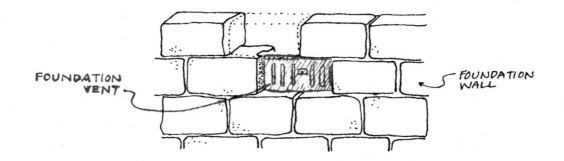

FOUNDATION VENT

FOUNDATION WALL

FOUNDATION WALL

Any wall which meets the ground and which supports the weight of the building above it may be called a foundation wall.

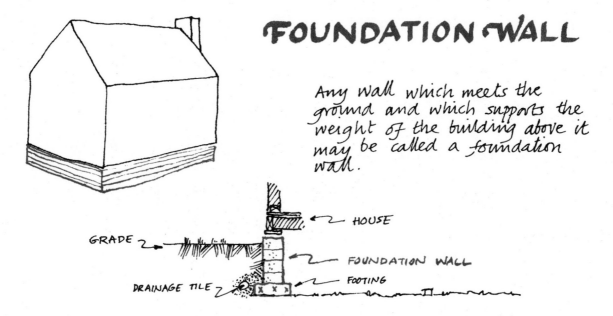

HOUSE

GRADE

FOUNDATION WALL

FOOTING

DRAINAGE TILE

FRAME

The frame of a house refers to the wooden skeleton (sometimes reinforced with steel) of a wood-framed house. This framing may be in one of several styles.

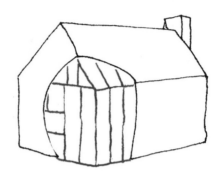

Many contemporary American houses are framed in the western or platform style (illustrated on page 100). This is a descendent and improvement of the so-called balloon style (illustrated on page 102) because it is both stronger and more fireproof (in the western style the various sections are integrally separate and impede the spread of fire). The balloon style was a cheapening of the braced frame (illustrated on page 106) which was developed as it became more difficult to obtain heavy timbers for the earlier post and beam style - best exemplified by old wooden barns.

In recent years there has been a partial return to earlier framing styles in the form of a more modern plank and beam construction, made possible by the use of laminated beams and improved methods of insulation which no longer require studs every sixteen inches.

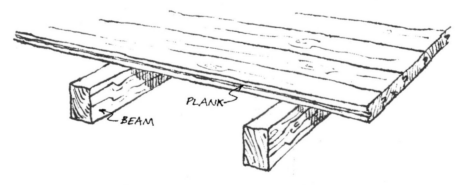

PLANK AND BEAM FRAMING

FRENCH WINDOW. see WINDOW

FRIEZE

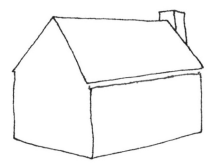

The classical frieze is that part of an entablature between the cornice and the architrave.

In modern houses the frieze is a horizontal board immediately below the cornice up against which the siding butts. Older American houses often made this board very wide, sometimes even wide enough for small windows.

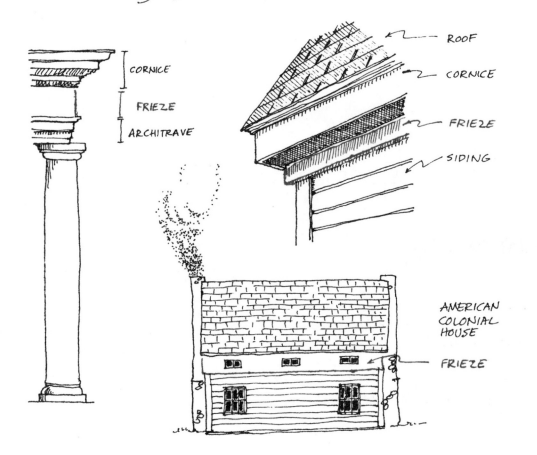

CORNICE

FRIEZE

ARCHITRAVE

ROOF

CORNICE

FRIEZE

SIDING

AMERICAN COLONIAL HOUSE

FRIEZE

FROST LINE

The frost line is the depth to which the ground can be expected to freeze. Since ground which freezes may move (often with incredible force), it is very important to start all foundations below this line in order to avoid heaving and possible collapse.

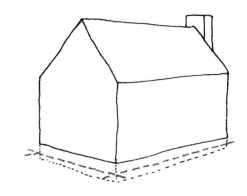

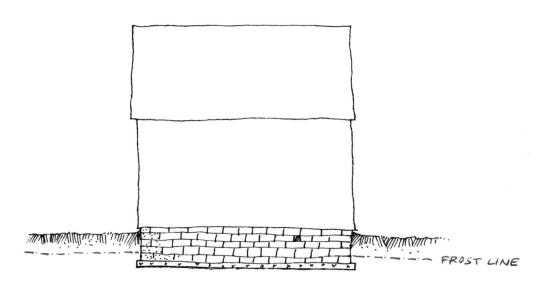

FROST LINE

FURNACE

A furnace is an enclosed chamber in which oil or some other combustible material is burned, for the purpose of heating air or water to heat a building. The furnace is usually in the basement.

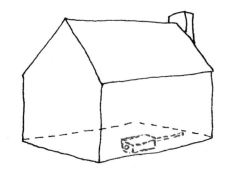

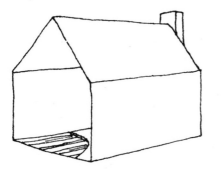

FURRING STRIPS

Sometimes spelled firring, furring strips are thin pieces of wood nailed on other timbers to make a level surface, such as on joists to make a level surface for the floorboards.

Also, when a concrete wall is to be paneled, furring strips are often first nailed to the wall with special masonry nails to provide a better nailing surface for the panels.

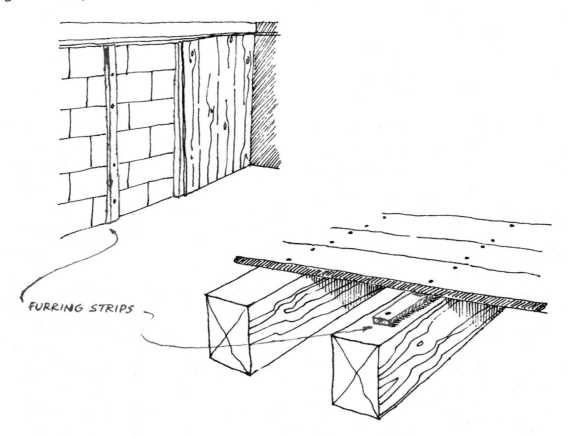

FURRING STRIPS

XV.

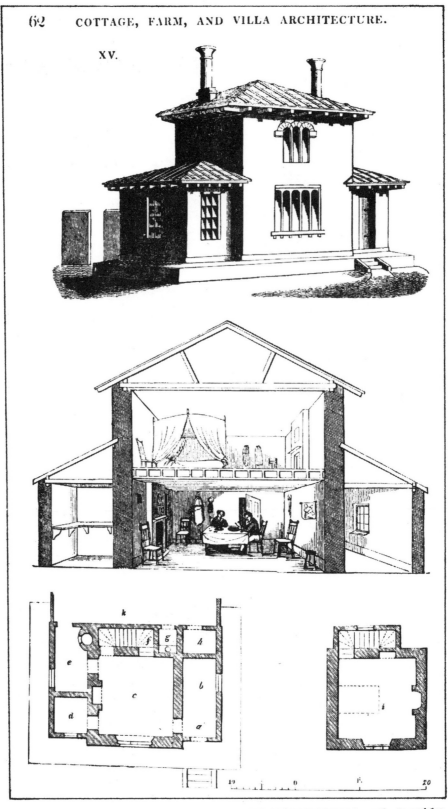

COTTAGE DWELLINGS   from AN ENCYCLOPÆDIA OF COTTAGE,
FARM AND VILLA   ARCHITECTURE by J.C. LOUDON, 1857

GABLE

The gable is the triangular part of a wall under a pitched roof, from the cornice to the peak. Gables are normally straight-sided, but there are also stepped gables and Dutch gables.

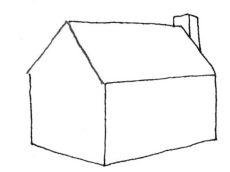

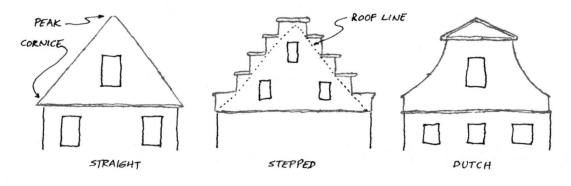

PEAK

CORNICE

ROOF LINE

STRAIGHT   STEPPED   DUTCH

THREE TYPES OF GABLE

GABLEBOARD. see BARGEBOARD

GABLE ROOF. see ROOF

GABLE VENT

Houses with uninsulated attics are usually built with screened louvers in the gables, which provide ventilation for the roof. Without these gable vents such roofs might be subject to damage from condensation.

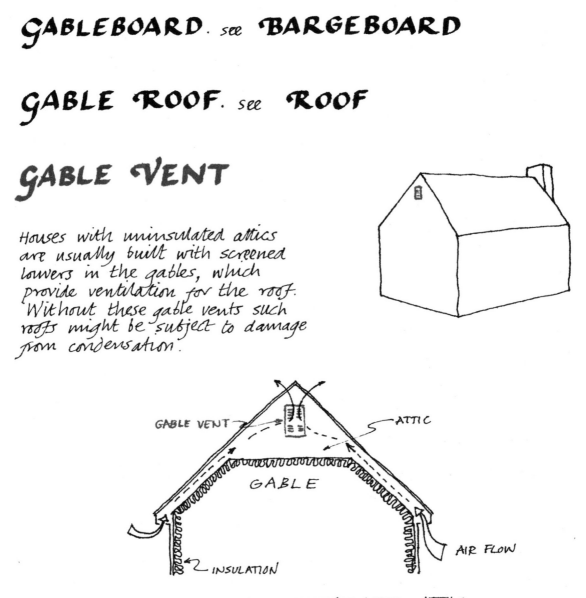

VENTILATION IN UNINSULATED ATTIC

GAMBREL ROOF. see ROOF

GARRET

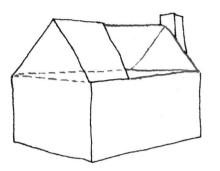

A garret is similar to an attic in that it is that part of the house on the upper floor, immediately under the roof. However, its derivation and origin is quite different. Garret comes from an old word meaning to guard, and originally signified a watch-tower built in the roof. (See also ATTIC.)

GIRDER

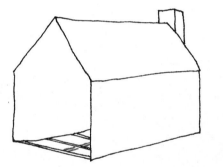

In a house, a girder refers to a main beam supporting the floor joists, which in turn support the flooring. The girder is usually supported by the foundation and its own piers.

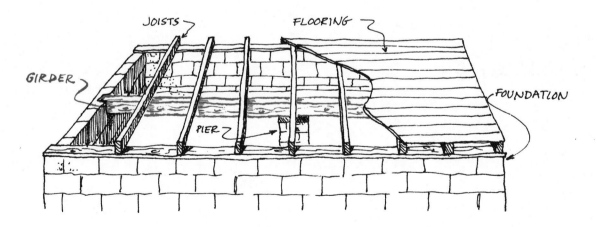

JOISTS   FLOORING
GIRDER   FOUNDATION
PIER

GIRT

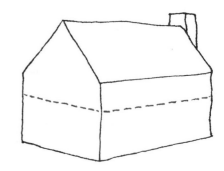

Girt is the name given to the horizontal beams in an old post-and-beam framed house which support the second level of floor joists, just as the sill supports the first or ground-floor level. Girts ran all round the house, and were known as front, rear, and end girts. In addition, there were two extra girts which ran from front to back, either side of the central chimney.

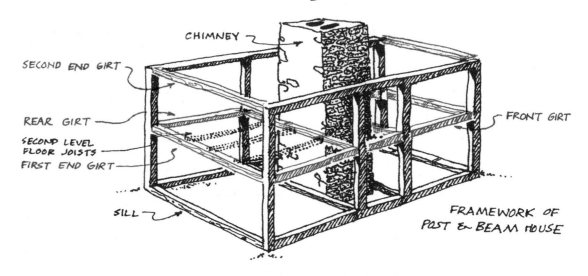

CHIMNEY

SECOND END GIRT

REAR GIRT

SECOND LEVEL
FLOOR JOISTS

FIRST END GIRT

FRONT GIRT

SILL

FRAMEWORK OF
POST & BEAM HOUSE

GRADE

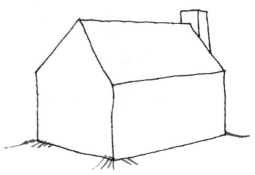

Grade is the term by which the level of the ground surrounding the house is known. 'Up to grade' means as high as the ground level; 'above grade' means above ground.

GROUNDS. *see* PLASTER GROUNDS

GUSSET

A gusset is a reinforcing plate of wood or metal which helps hold two pieces of wood together, as, for example, in the case of prefabricated rafter trusses which are held together by metal gussets.

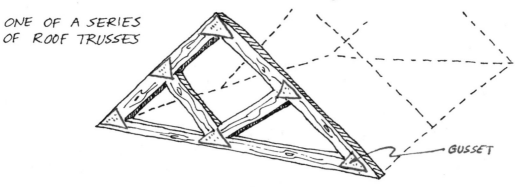

ONE OF A SERIES OF ROOF TRUSSES

GUSSET

GUTTER

A gutter is a channel fixed at the edge of a roof to collect and lead away water. Commonly made from galvanized metal, gutters are also made from wood and may even be an integral part of a masonry wall.

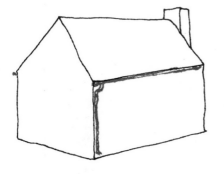

SECTION OF REDWOOD GUTTER

9 3

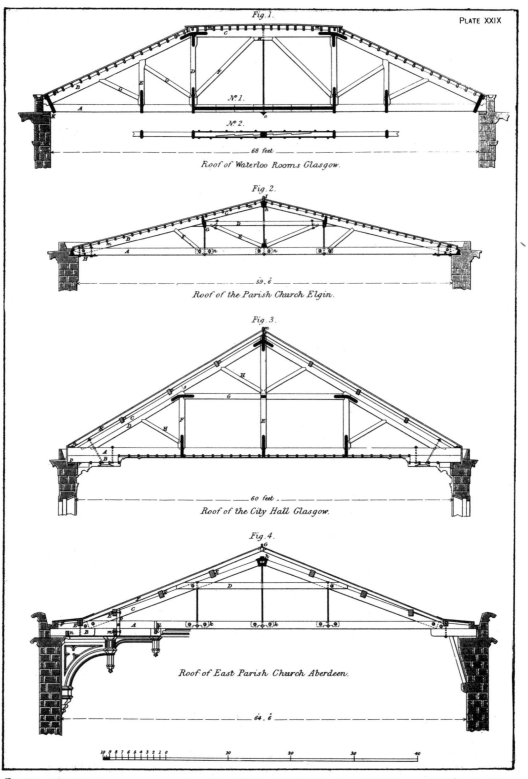

PLATE XXIX

Fig. 1.

Nº 1.

Nº 2.

68 feet

Roof of Waterloo Rooms Glasgow.

Fig. 2.

59.6

Roof of the Parish Church Elgin.

Fig. 3.

60 feet

Roof of the City Hall Glasgow.

Fig. 4.

Roof of East Parish Church Aberdeen.

64.6

ROOF TRUSSES   from THE MODERN CARPENTER JOINER AND
CABINET-MAKER by G. LISTER SUTCLIFFE, 1903

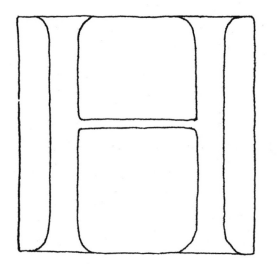

HANDRAIL

A handrail is a rail to hold on to, typically when ascending and descending staircases. A staircase handrail commonly ends at a newel and is supported by balusters, but simpler handrails may be attached to an adjacent wall by brackets.

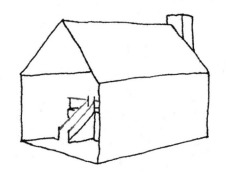

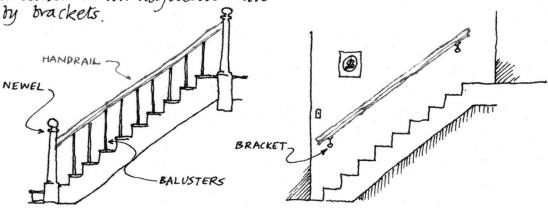

HANDRAIL

NEWEL

BALUSTERS

BRACKET

HANGER

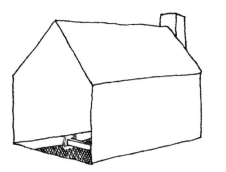

Hangers are metal straps so designed as to support the ends of timbers, such as joists, used when there is no time to make proper joints.

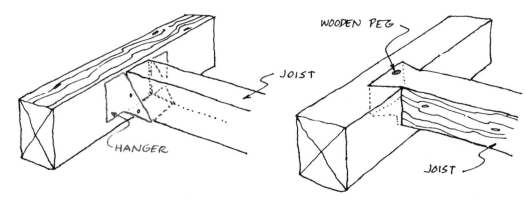

JOIST

HANGER

WOODEN PEG

JOIST

PEGGED JOINT

HEAD

The head is the top horizontal member of a door or window casing. (The side pieces are called jambs.)

ARCHITRAVE

DOOR

HEAD

JAMB } CASING

HEADER

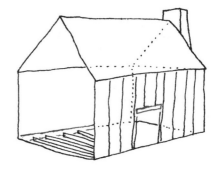

1. Header is the name given to the timber that runs in the same plane as, but at right angles to, the joists of a house. The header is nailed to the ends of the joists. (See also **DOUBLE HEADER**.)

2. Header is also the name given to the horizontal framing member over a rough opening for a door or window. This header is always spoken of as singular even though in light wood framing it is invariably made up of two pieces of wood nailed together.

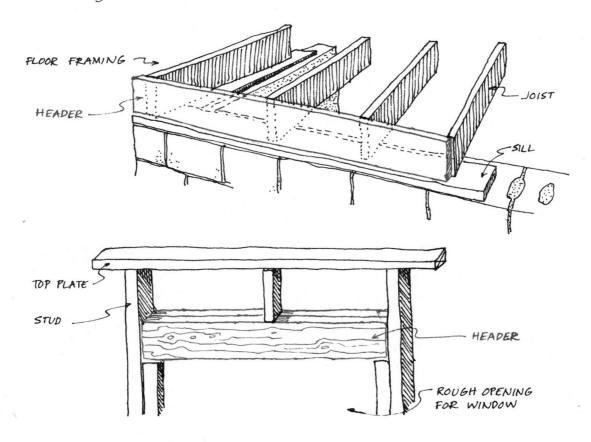

FLOOR FRAMING

HEADER

JOIST

SILL

TOP PLATE

STUD

HEADER

ROUGH OPENING FOR WINDOW

HEARTH

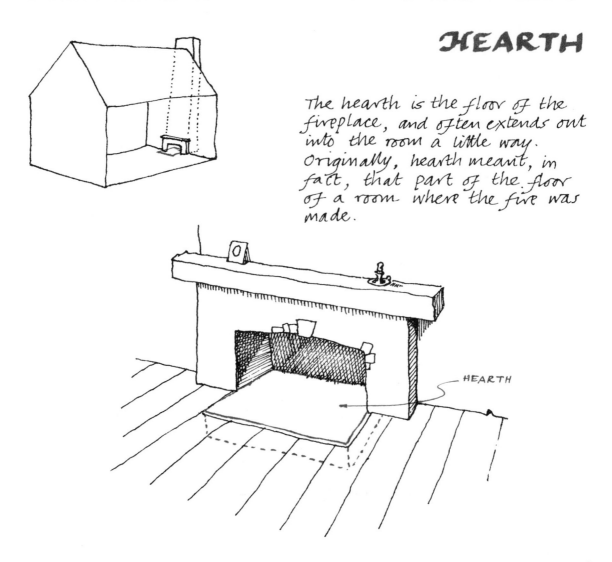

The hearth is the floor of the fireplace, and often extends out into the room a little way. Originally, hearth meant, in fact, that part of the floor of a room where the fire was made.

HEARTH

HINGE

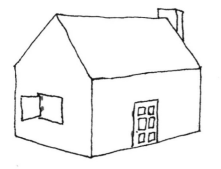

A hinge is the joint or mechanism by which a door or window is made to open and close. The word comes from 'hang,' and the process of fixing hinges is still known as hanging a door or a window. A hinge which closes like a sandwich is known as a butt (the two leaves butt up against each other).

HIP

The hip is the external angle formed by the meeting of two slopes of a roof. In this basic sense hip is sometimes the same as 'peak' which refers to the topmost line of a roof. However, a hip roof is not simply a roof with a hip, but rather a roof whose ends are also slanted, having at least three hips.

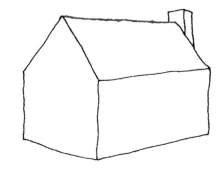

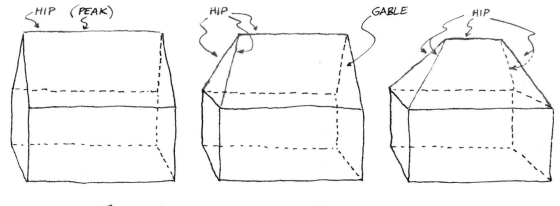

GABLE ROOF (ONE HIP)   HIP AND GABLE ROOF   HIP ROOF
                         (THREE HIPS)   (FIVE HIPS)

HIP AND VALLEY ROOF. see ROOF

HIP ROOF. see ROOF

BELMONT COLLEGE LIBRARY

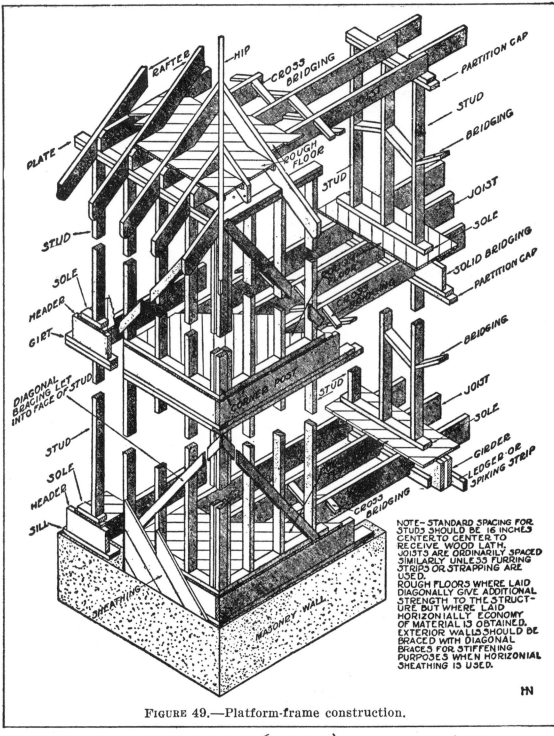

The following labels appear on the illustration:

RAFTER · HIP · CROSS BRIDGING · PARTITION CAP · STUD · BRIDGING · PLATE · ROUGH FLOOR · JOIST · STUD · SOLE · STUD · SOLID BRIDGING · PARTITION CAP · SOLE · HEADER · GIRT · DIAGONAL BRACING LET INTO FACE OF STUD · CORNER POST · STUD · BRIDGING · JOIST · SOLE · STUD · GIRDER · LEDGER OR SPIKING STRIP · SOLE · HEADER · CROSS BRIDGING · SILL · SHEATHING · MASONRY WALL

NOTE— STANDARD SPACING FOR STUDS SHOULD BE 16 INCHES CENTER TO CENTER TO RECEIVE WOOD LATH. JOISTS ARE ORDINARILY SPACED SIMILARLY UNLESS FURRING STRIPS OR STRAPPING ARE USED.
ROUGH FLOORS WHERE LAID DIAGONALLY GIVE ADDITIONAL STRENGTH TO THE STRUCTURE BUT WHERE LAID HORIZONIALLY ECONOMY OF MATERIAL IS OBTAINED. EXTERIOR WALLS SHOULD BE BRACED WITH DIAGONAL BRACES FOR STIFFENING PURPOSES WHEN HORIZONIAL SHEATHING IS USED.

HN

FIGURE 49.—Platform-frame construction.

HOUSE FRAMING, WESTERN STYLE (PLATFORM)   from WOOD HANDBOOK by R.F. LUXFORD and GEORGE W. TRAYLER, 1940

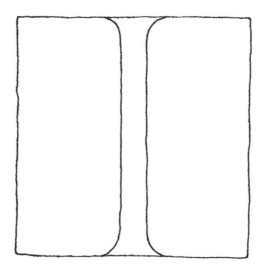

INSULATION

Insulation is anything that prevents or reduces heat trans-ference from one area to another. Almost all houses need it one way or another, either to retain the heat produced in the house in winter, or to keep the summer heat from penetrating a house cooled by an air conditioner.

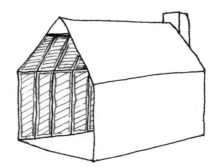

Insulation comes in many forms, from dead air space created by double windows, to fiberglass batts or foil-backed rolls inserted between the framing studs of a house, and to various foams sprayed onto and into the walls, roofs, and floors of a house.

INTERIOR WALL . see WALL

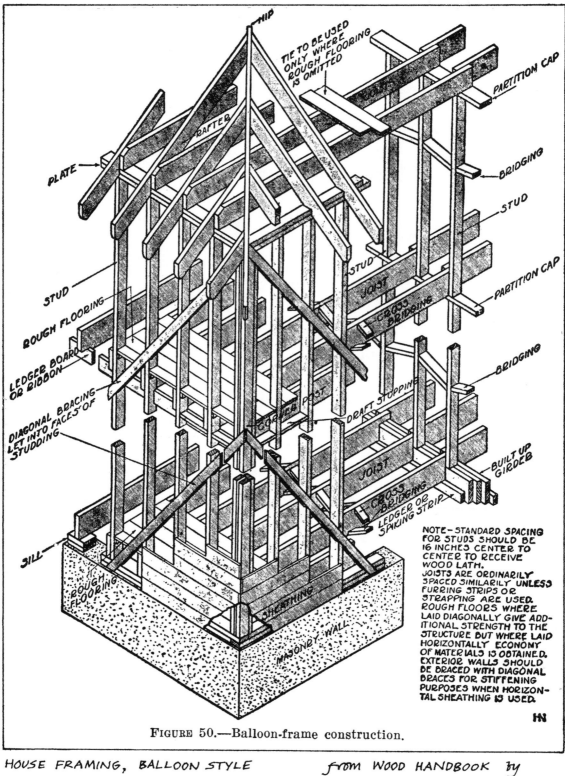

FIGURE 50.—Balloon-frame construction.

HOUSE FRAMING, BALLOON STYLE   from WOOD HANDBOOK by
R.F. LUXFORD and GEORGE W. TRAYLER, 1940

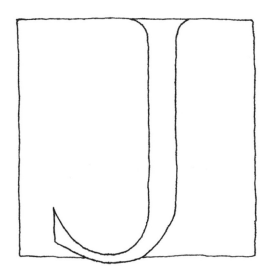

JACK RAFTER

A jack rafter is a rafter which is shorter than a full-length rafter (one that stretches from the eaves to the peak). Jack rafters occur in hip roofs where the top edge of a roof slope is not horizontal, and in roofs with valleys.

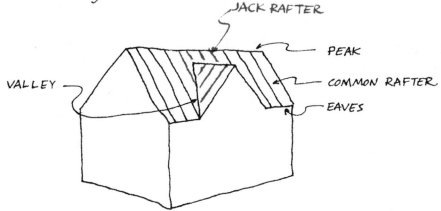

JACK RAFTER

VALLEY

PEAK

COMMON RAFTER

EAVES

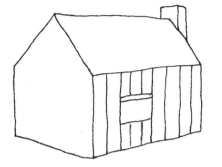

JACK STUD

A stud is one of the upright framing members in a wood-framed house, and a jack stud is one of these members which does not reach all the way from the bottom plate to the top plate, being intercepted by some other member. (A stud which does not reach all the way from the top plate to the bottom plate is properly called a cripple stud.)

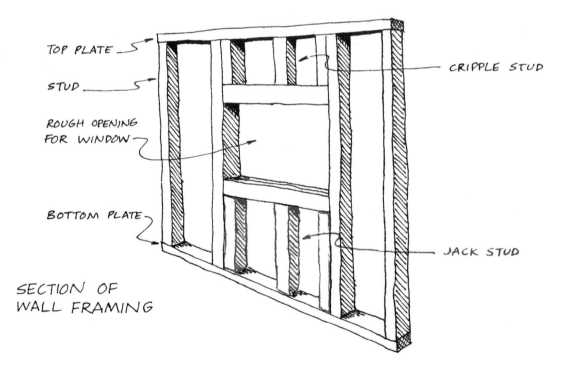

TOP PLATE

STUD

ROUGH OPENING
FOR WINDOW

BOTTOM PLATE

CRIPPLE STUD

JACK STUD

SECTION OF
WALL FRAMING

JALOUSIE. see WINDOW

JAMB

Jamb is a word which derives from the French for 'leg,' and refers to the vertical side of any opening, typically the upright part of a door or a window casing. In the case of a door or a casement window, the two jambs are differentiated as hinge jamb and lock jamb.

HINGE JAMB   LOCK JAMB

JOIST

The word joist derives from the Latin word meaning 'to lie,' and refers to a horizontal timber which supports the boards of a floor (and sometimes, if it is a second-floor joist, the ceiling of the room below). (see illustration facing page 71.)

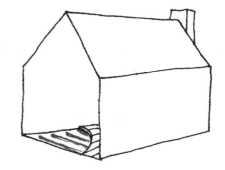

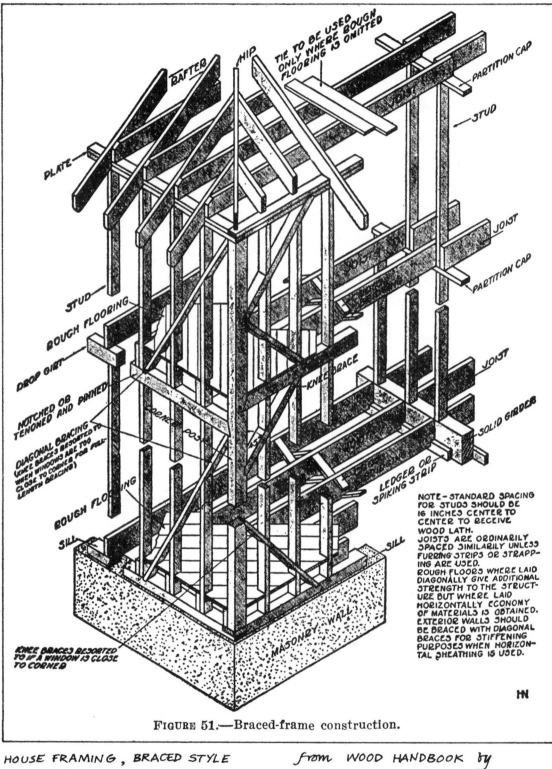

FIGURE 51.—Braced-frame construction.

HOUSE FRAMING, BRACED STYLE   from WOOD HANDBOOK by
R.F. LUXFORD and GEORGE W. TRAYLER, 1940

KING POST

The king post is the wood post (or metal rod) which extends from the apex of two joined rafters to the center of the tie beam which connects their feet, and which forms thus a truss.

KING POST

RAFTER

TIE BEAM

KNEE WALL

A knee wall is a vertical wall which, by reason of a sloping roof, does not extend all the way from floor to ceiling, but is often only 'knee high'.

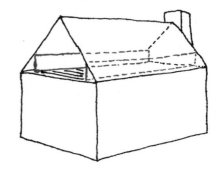

Front Doors.

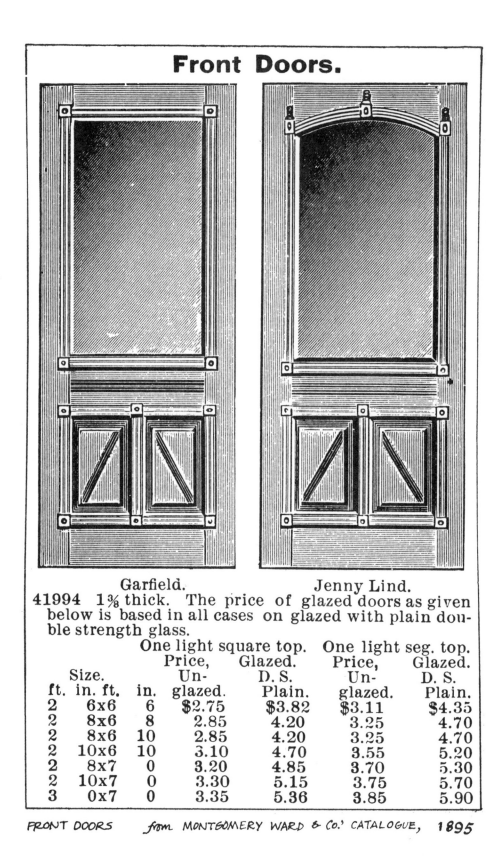

Garfield.   Jenny Lind.

41994 1⅜ thick. The price of glazed doors as given below is based in all cases on glazed with plain double strength glass.

Size.			One light square top.		One light seg. top.	
			Price, Un-glazed.	Glazed. D. S. Plain.	Price, Un-glazed.	Glazed. D. S. Plain.
ft.	in. ft.	in.				
2	6x6	6	$2.75	$3.82	$3.11	$4.35
2	8x6	8	2.85	4.20	3.25	4.70
2	8x6	10	2.85	4.20	3.25	4.70
2	10x6	10	3.10	4.70	3.55	5.20
2	8x7	0	3.20	4.85	3.70	5.30
2	10x7	0	3.30	5.15	3.75	5.70
3	0x7	0	3.35	5.36	3.85	5.90

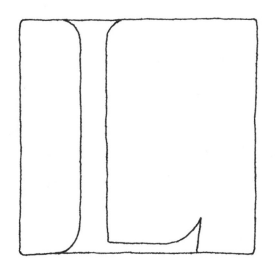

LANDING

The landing is the first part of
a floor at the head of a flight
of stairs, or the resting place
between two flights.

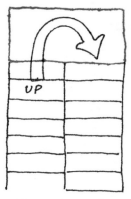

HALF LANDING

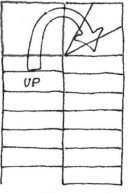

QUARTER LANDING

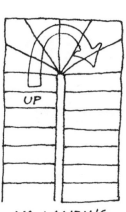

NO LANDING

LATH

A lath is a thin strip of wood (typically white pine, though early American lathing was made from green (unseasoned) oak), which is nailed to a wall or ceiling and over which plaster is applied. Nowadays, wooden laths have been largely replaced by perforated metal sheets, (called wire lath) to which plaster is applied.

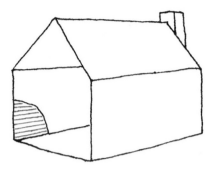

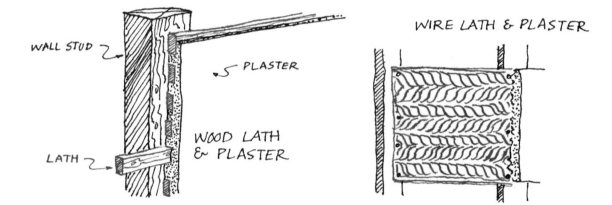

WALL STUD

PLASTER

WOOD LATH & PLASTER

LATH

WIRE LATH & PLASTER

LEADER . see DOWNSPOUT

LEDGER

A ledger is a piece of wood nailed to a vertical surface so as to provide a ledge on which something else, such as a joist, may rest.

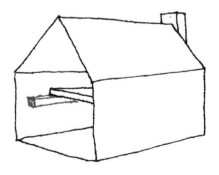

LIGHT

In reference to a house, light means the glass in windows and doors. A window with six panes of glass is called a six-light window. Three panes is a three-light window, and so on.

LINTEL

Lintel is a word which over the centuries has completely reversed its meaning. It started out as the Latin word 'limen,' which means threshold – the piece of wood or stone that forms the bottom of a doorway and over which one must cross to enter the house. As Latin spread and a popular Latin evolved in the further reaches of the Empire, 'limen' became confused with 'limit' (which means limit or border) and which, in turn, passed into Old French as 'lintel.' By the time 'lintel' was established in English it had become the word not for the bottom of a doorway but the top.

Nowadays, a lintel is any horizontal piece of timber or stone placed over an opening to carry the weight above.

LIMEN
CLASSICAL LATIN

LIMIT
POPULAR LATIN

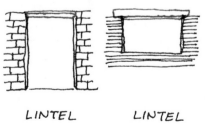

LINTEL
OLD FRENCH

LINTEL
ENGLISH

COAD CENTER

Load center is a name sometimes given to the box, often found in the basement or under the stairs, which houses the fuses or circuit breakers. It is actually the distribution point in the house for the main electricity supply and is connected directly to the main supply outside.

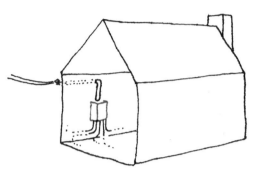

COOKOUT

A lookout is a short timber support for an overhanging roof at a gable.

The word is also used to describe a short piece of wood connecting the tail of a rafter to the side of the house, thereby providing somewhere to nail the soffit to.

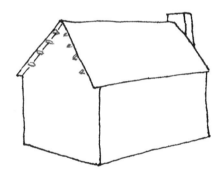

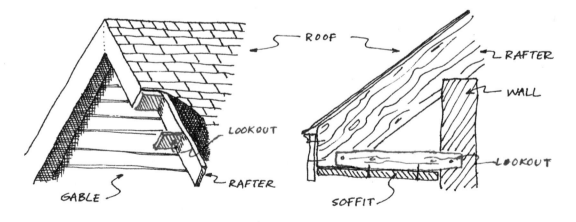

ROOF

RAFTER

WALL

LOOKOUT

LOOKOUT

RAFTER

GABLE

SOFFIT

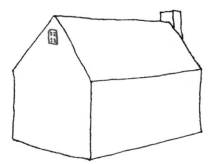

COUVER

A louver is an arrangement of inclined horizontal slats in an opening which admit air but not rain or light. A door or window fitted with such slats is a louvered door or window. Louvered (unglazed) windows (fitted with screens to exclude insects) are often used to ventilate attic areas in roofs.

The word comes from a small medieval domed turret (known as a louver (even in British English) which later acquired the slats which subsequently stole the name.

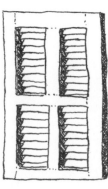

MODERN LOUVER

MEDIEVAL LOUVER

Roofing Felts and Papers.

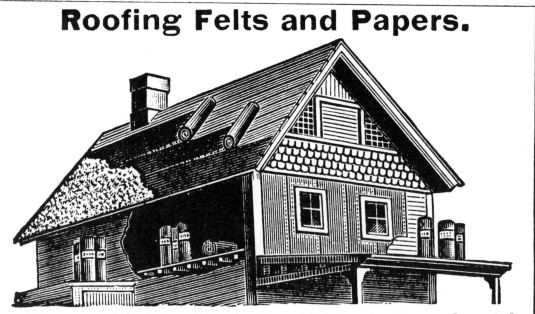

We are selling immense quantities of our roofing felt and papers and they are everywhere giving excellent satisfaction. Our prepared roofing felt is adapted for either flat or steep roofs, is suitable for all climates and not affected by severe winters.

It is easy to apply, and when coated with our asphaltum cement is not injured by steam, acids or gases, which are so destructive to tin and metal roofs. It is used extensively for covering roofs of factories, warehouses, barns, residences and all farm buildings. In fact everywhere where a good roof is required at a low price. No other tools than a jack knife, hammer and a brush are necessary to apply it. Complete directions with each roll. We put in 2 gallons cement with each roll, which is enough for two coats. Our 2 and 3-ply felt is 32 in. wide, about 40 feet long and put up in rolls containing 108 squarefeet. Every roll, allowing for lap, will cover 100 square feet, or a space 10 feet by 10 feet. Price includes, with each roll, 2 gallons cement, 1½ pounds tin caps, 1½ pound barbed roofing nails.

42035 2-Ply Roofing Felt. Weight, about 75 pounds per roll. Price, with cement, caps and nails.
Per roll..$1.60

42036 3-Ply Roofing Felt. Weight about 100 pounds per roll. Price, complete with cement, caps and nails. Per roll......................... 1.90

ROOFING MATERIALS *from* MONTGOMERY WARD & CO.' CATALOGUE, 1895

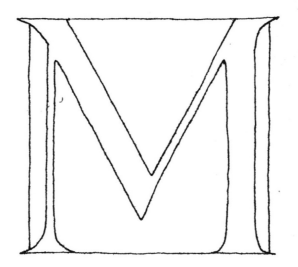

MANSARD ROOF. see ROOF

MANTELPIECE

The mantelpiece is all the ornamental structure of wood, stone, or other material, which surrounds a fireplace. The mantelshelf is a horizontal board fixed in this structure, formerly frequently draped.

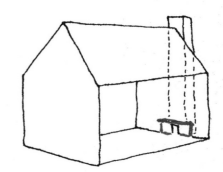

VICTORIAN MANTELPIECE

MANTELSHELF

MASONRY

Masonry refers to all that work in and around a house done by a mason – a worker in stone. While many houses are constructed almost entirely by masons, the typical American wood-frame house generally only has a masonry foundation and chimney.

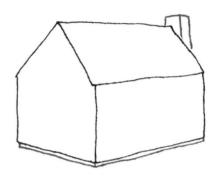

MOULDING

A moulding is a curved section formed in the edge or face of wood and stone chiefly for the sake of ornament. In wood-work the moulding has become a separate piece of wood (referred to as a planted moulding, in distinction to a stuck moulding which is formed on solid wood) and is now most frequently used to fill corners (see ARCHITRAVE, BASEBOARD SHOE, BED MOULDING, CROWN MOULDING, etc.). Mouldings may be classified by their purpose, e.g. bed, crown, shingle, etc., or according to their design, e.g. cove, ogee, quarter-round, etc.

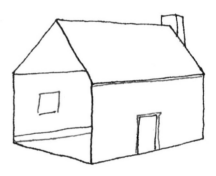

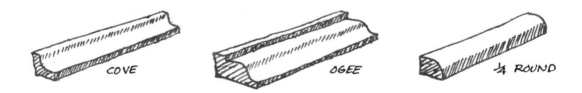

COVE   OGEE   ¼ ROUND

THREE COMMON MOULDINGS

MULLION

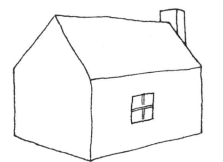

A mullion is one of the vertical members of a window, dividing the glass — such a window is often called a mullioned window.

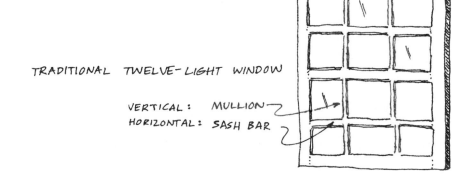

TRADITIONAL TWELVE-LIGHT WINDOW

VERTICAL : MULLION
HORIZONTAL : SASH BAR

MUNTIN

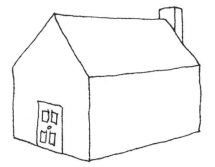

A muntin is an intermediate member of a door's framework separating the panels and butting into the rails.

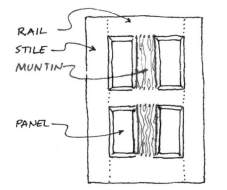

RAIL
STILE
MUNTIN

PANEL

FOUR-PANELED DOOR

19TH CENTURY BRITISH WOODCUT

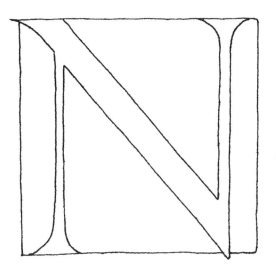

NAILER

A nailer is any small piece of wood fixed to a larger to provide a nailing surface for another piece of wood or sheetrock (or anything else which needs be nailed).

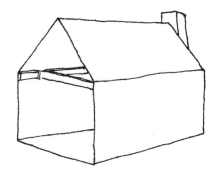

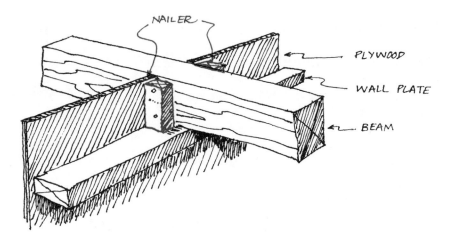

NAILER

PLYWOOD

WALL PLATE

BEAM

NEWEL

Newel has two similar meanings: one is the upright post or cylinder around which a circular staircase turns; and two is the upright post which receives the handrails of a staircase.

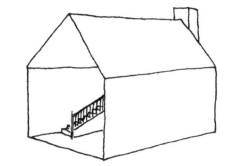

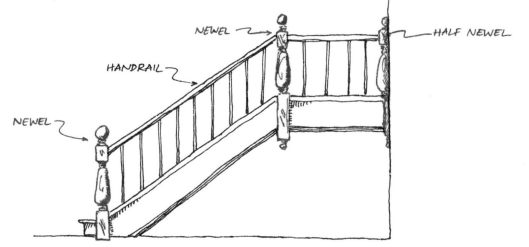

NEWEL

HALF NEWEL

HANDRAIL

NEWEL

NOGGING

Nogging is an old term describing the brickwork built up between the timbers of a house's frame. The main posts are called the quarters, and the horizontal timbers which connect and strengthen the quarters are called nogging pieces.

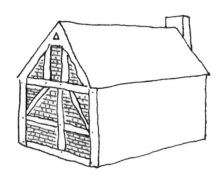

NOSING

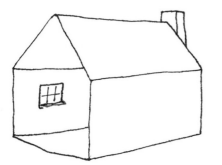

A nosing is a projecting edge of a board, such as the edge of a stair step (tread), or the front of a window sill. The actual nosing may be square, rounded, or otherwise moulded.

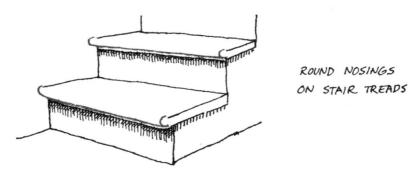

ROUND NOSINGS ON STAIR TREADS

MOULDED NOSING ON WINDOW SILL

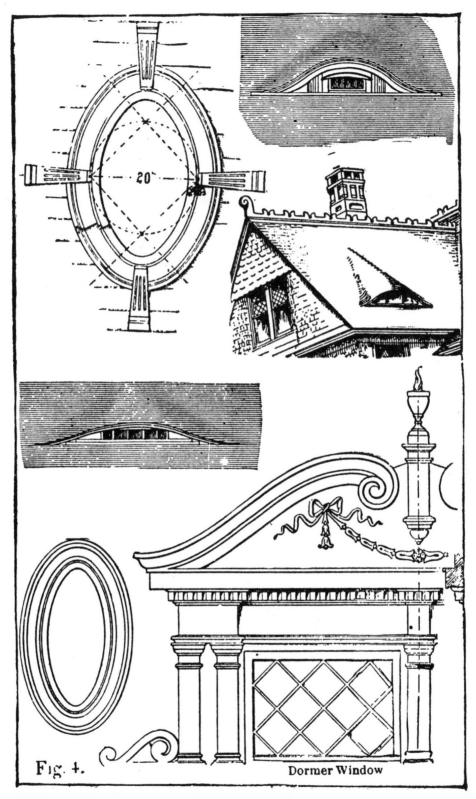

Fig. 4.

Dormer Window

OVAL WINDOWS & DORMER WINDOWS (INCLUDING THREE
EYEBROW DORMERS   from MODERN CARPENTRY, A
PRACTICAL MANUAL by FRED T. HODGSON, 1902

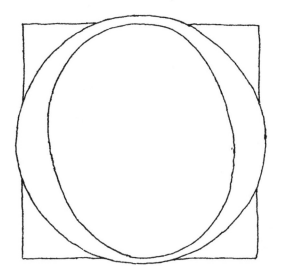

ORIEL. see WINDOW

OUTLET SEWER

Outlet sewer is the name given
to the pipe that drains the liquid
from a septic tank, after the
sediment has sunk to the bottom,
and leads it to the distribution
box whence it is percolated out
over the drainage field.

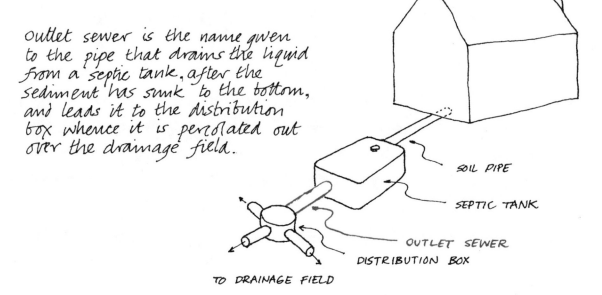

SOIL PIPE

SEPTIC TANK

OUTLET SEWER
DISTRIBUTION BOX

TO DRAINAGE FIELD

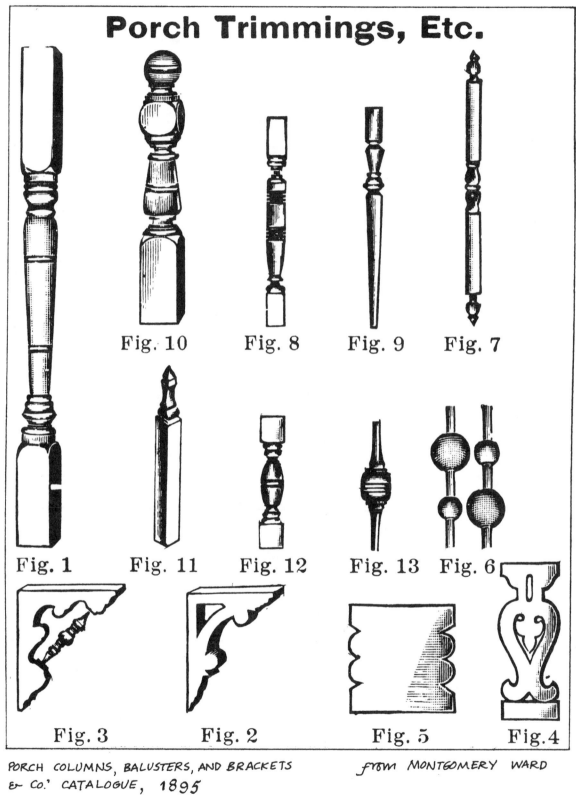

Porch Trimmings, Etc.

Fig. 10

Fig. 8

Fig. 9

Fig. 7

Fig. 1

Fig. 11

Fig. 12

Fig. 13

Fig. 6

Fig. 3

Fig. 2

Fig. 5

Fig. 4

PORCH COLUMNS, BALUSTERS, AND BRACKETS
& CO. CATALOGUE, 1895

from MONTGOMERY WARD

PALLET

A pallet is a piece of wood the same thickness as a mortar joint set into the masonry, around a rough opening for a door, to provide something into which the door casing may be screwed.

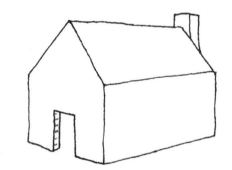

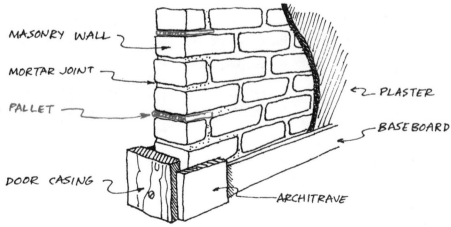

MASONRY WALL

MORTAR JOINT

PALLET

PLASTER

BASEBOARD

DOOR CASING

ARCHITRAVE

PANEL BOX

Panel box is one of several names given to the fuse or circuit breaker box found in most houses, usually located under the stairs or in the basement. What is immediately visible when the door is opened is a 'panel' of switches which control the flow of electricity around the house.

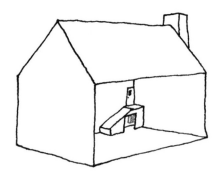

PANELING

Paneling now means the covering of an interior wall with any kind of wood. It used to imply the use of wood made into a series of framed panels – like a paneled door, but it now includes the use of sheets of plywood 'paneling,' and even simple strips of wood.

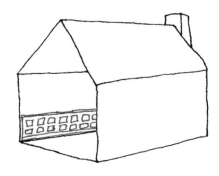

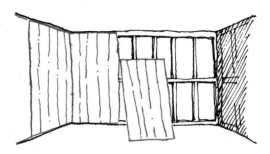

ROOM BEING FINISHED WITH
PLYWOOD PANELING

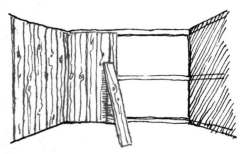

ROOM BEING FINISHED WITH
PLANKS OF KNOTTY PINE

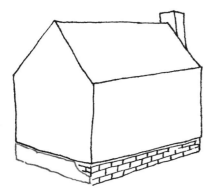

PARGING

Originally 'pargeting' (from the French 'par' meaning over, and 'jeter' meaning to throw), parging means to apply a rough coat of mortar or plaster for protection or as a finish. The inside of brick chimney flues used to be pargeted. Nowadays, concrete block foundations are parged as a base for an asphaltic waterproofing compound.

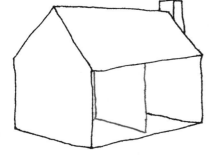

PARTITION

Partition is a term applied to an interior wall which divides two rooms. A partition may be a simple 'curtain wall,' meaning that it carries no load, or a 'bearing wall,' meaning that it forms an integral part of the building's structure and supports something – the roof or another floor.

PEAK

The peak is the highest part of
a roof. Strictly, the peak
refers to the top of a gable, but
it is also used synonymously
with the ridge - the juncture
of two roof slopes.

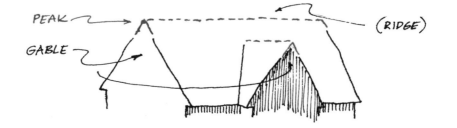

PICTURE RAIL

The picture rail is a horizontal
moulding which runs around a
room just below the ceiling,
from which pictures may be
hung. It also used to be used as
the upper limit of wallpaper,
the short space above being
decorated like the ceiling and
known as the frieze.

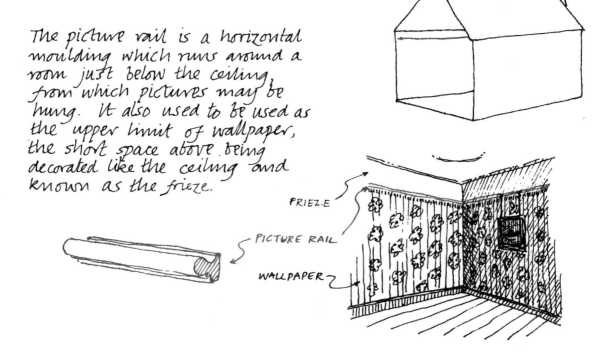

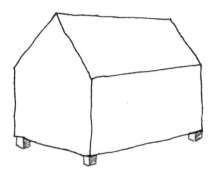

STUMP PIER

Pier is technically the support for one of the arches of a bridge, but in American it is now also used to describe the columnar supports of a house known in British as a stump. In fact, houses are said to be built either on a full foundation (meaning footings and a foundation wall) or on (a series of) piers. Piers may be made of stone, wood, or concrete. Piers may also be used inside a full foundation (see GIRDER).

THREE KINDS OF PIERS

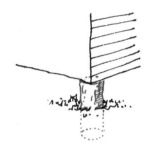

LOCUST POST PIER

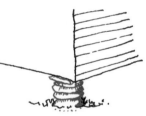

DRY STONE PIER

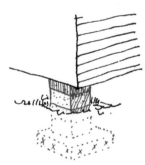

CONCRETE BLOCK PIER

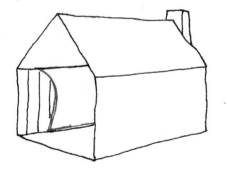

PLASTER

Plaster is a mixture of lime and sand which is applied in a wet, plastic state to interior surfaces and which then hardens. Before the invention of sheetrock, houses which boasted any interior finish were either paneled or plastered.

PLASTER GROUNDS

Plaster grounds are narrow strips of wood applied around areas to be plastered in order to provide a leveling surface and a plaster stop for the plaster. Along the floor line they also provide a nailing surface for the baseboard.

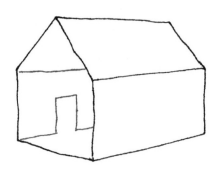

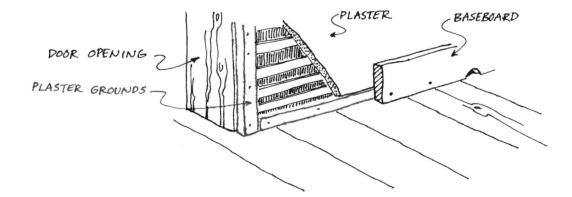

PLATE

Plate is the general term for any horizontal timber in a wall which receives the ends of vertical members. In wood-frame construction they are referred to as the top (or rafter) plate, and the bottom (or sole or shoe or toe) plate.

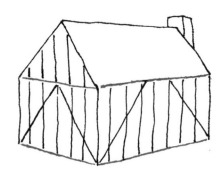

PLUG

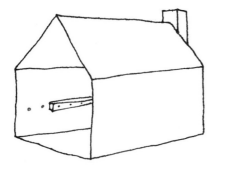

A **plug** is a small piece of wood inserted into a masonry wall, usually into the mortar joint, in order to provide somewhere to nail or screw some subsequently superimposed covering, such as a door casing, furring strips, or plaster grounds.

MORTAR JOINT →

MASONRY WALL →

← PLUG

← FURRING STRIP

PLUMBING

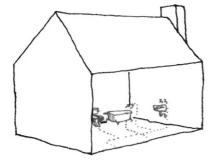

The plumbing of a house includes everything to do with water — drains, waterlines, and fixtures. This curious word comes originally from the Latin for lead — out of which water pipes used to be made until it was discovered that lead is poisonous.

PORCH

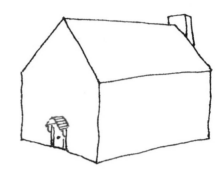

A porch is a covered entrance to a building; if it is supported by columns it is properly called a portico. The term is also used in America to denote any covered, and often screened-in but otherwise open, area outside the house. Such a structure is, however, really a veranda and not a porch.

PORCH (PORTICO)   VERANDA

POST

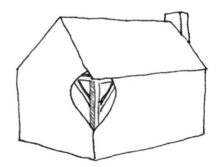

A post is an upright timber (in distinction to a horizontal timber, which is known as a beam). The word post has many uses, not only to do with framing, such as doorpost, queen post, king post, etc.

132

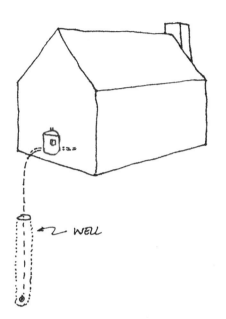

PRESSURE TANK

A pressure tank is a necessary part of a house which gets its water from a well. The water is pumped up into the pressure tank from where it is drawn as needed. When water leaves the pressure tank, the pressure drops and activates a relay which starts the pump working, bringing more water up from the well and thus ensuring a constant supply.

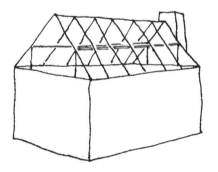

PURLIN

A purlin is a horizontal roof member which runs at right angles to the rafters and helps to support them.

PYRAMID ROOF. see ROOF

HOUSE

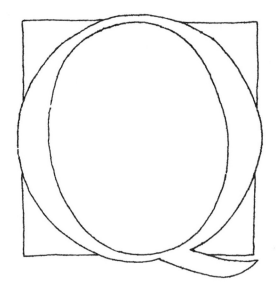

QUEEN POST

A queen post is one of a pair
of posts used in heavy
timbered roof construction. The
queen posts are placed symetric-
ally on the tie beam (or a
collar beam) and lend support
to the rafters immediately
above.

RAFTER

QUEEN POST

TIE BEAM

RADIATOR

In a house, a radiator is understood to be an arrangement of metal pipes carrying hot water, designed to give off, or radiate, the heat and so warm the house.

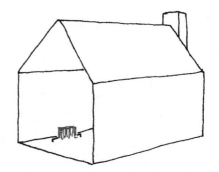

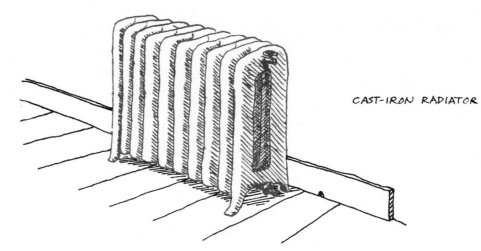

CAST-IRON RADIATOR

RAFTER

A rafter is one of the timbers which provide the slope and support for a roof and which carry the shingles, tiles, slates, or any other outer covering. There are various kinds of rafters, classified according to their position in the roof, such as common, hip, jack, or valley rafters.

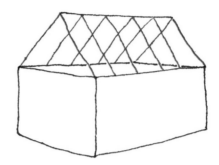

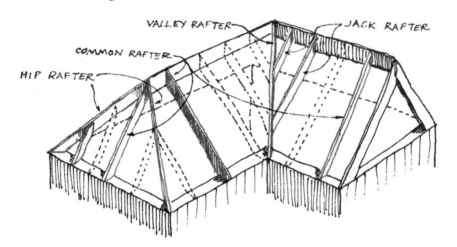

RAFTER TAIL

The rafter tail is that part of the rafter which overhangs the wall on which the bottom of the rafter rests. Note, not all rafters are made with tails, some rafters finish at the wall and there is thus no roof overhang at all.

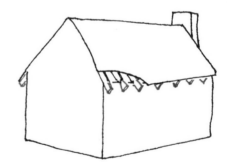

RAGLIN

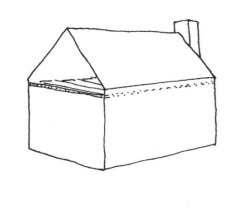

Raglin is a term used in the north of England for a ceiling joist which does not support any floor above it, and is consequently a relatively light-weight timber.

RAKE

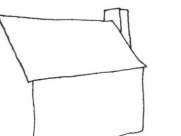

Rake really means slope or inclination, but since a roof, when viewed from the gable end, necessarily slopes, this part of the roof, when it overhangs the gable, is referred to as the rake. The rake is supported by lookouts (see LOOKOUT).

REGISTER

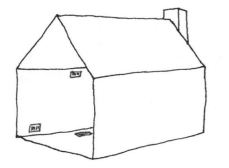

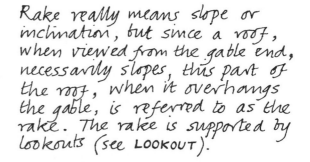

Register is the name given to the grill set in the floor or wall through which hot (or cold) air is pushed in a house with hot air heating. A register, by definition, may also be opened and closed, or at least regulated.

RETAINING WALL. see WALL

REVEAL

The space between a door frame
and the wall in which it is
set is known as the reveal.

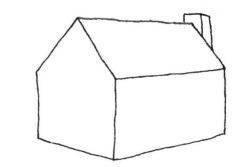

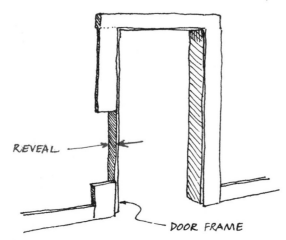

REVEAL

DOOR FRAME

RIDGE

The ridge is the topmost part of a
roof where two slopes join — the
topmost part of the gable (at
the end of the ridge) is known
as the peak. The two terms
are often confused.

PEAK
GABLE

RIDGE

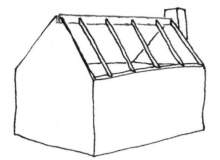

RIDGE BEAM
RIDGE BOARD
RIDGE POLE

All three terms indicate the same member in a roof's framework — the topmost horizontal piece which supports and connects the upper ends of the rafters. The difference lies in the size of the timbers used — ridge beam implying a heavy timber as was common in heavy timbered frame buildings; ridge pole implying a single pole used in rough construction; and ridge board implying the use of a regular plank. Actually, early buildings very often dispensed with any kind of ridge and simply joined the rafters to each other with wooden pins. Nowadays, common usage mixes all three terms.

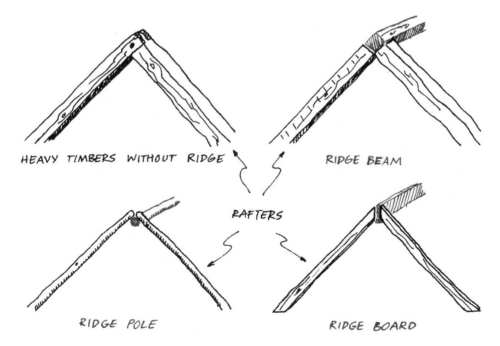

HEAVY TIMBERS WITHOUT RIDGE

RIDGE BEAM

RAFTERS

RIDGE POLE

RIDGE BOARD

139

RIDGE VENT

In order to avoid the dangers of condensation, a roof must be properly ventilated, especially if insulated. One way of achieving this without sacrificing needed space in the roof is to use a vent which is installed in the actual ridge, or top of the roof.

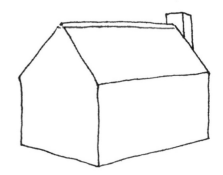

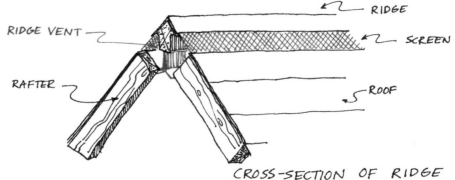

CROSS-SECTION OF RIDGE SHOWING RIDGE VENT

RISER

A riser is the vertical part of a step in a staircase (though not all stairs have risers).

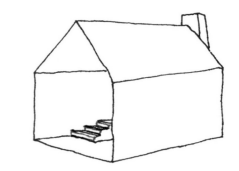

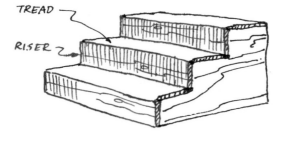

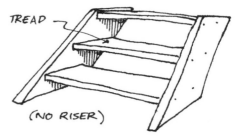

(NO RISER)

140

ROOF

The roof is the upper outside covering of a building and may consist of a variety of materials such as thatch, tin, wood shingles, clay tiles, asphalt or tar, and stone.

Just as there are many materials for roofs so are there many designs, some of which are shown below.

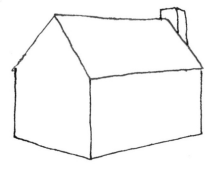

GABLE OR SADDLEBACK ROOF

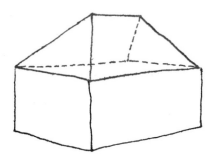

HIP OR HIPPED ROOF

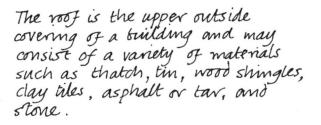

GAMBREL ROOF

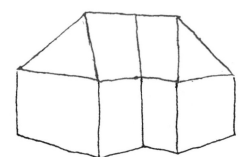

HIP AND VALLEY ROOF

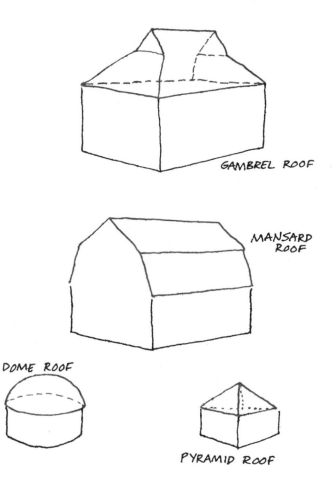

MANSARD ROOF

DOME ROOF

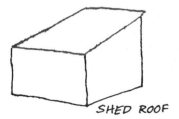

SHED ROOF

PYRAMID ROOF

ROOF BOARDS

Roof boards are horizontal boards, nailed onto the rafters, to which the outer roof covering (whatever it may be) is nailed. In many cases nowadays, plywood is used although roofboards are still best for wood shingles as they allow the shingles to breathe.

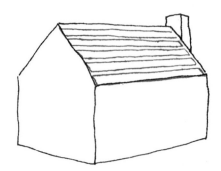

ROOFING TIN

A roofing tin is a small round disc, made of shiny metal (which, however, soon rusts) about the size of a silver dollar or an old half-crown, through which a roofing nail is hammered when building paper is being applied. If the building paper is to be covered immediately by some other material it is more efficient to staple it down. But if the paper is to remain exposed to the wind for any length of time then the roofing tin will help prevent it from tearing.

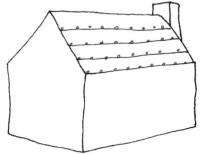

ROOFING TIN

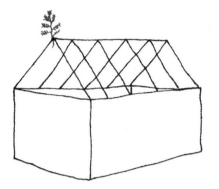

ROOF TREE

A vestige of ancient builders' rites, the roof tree, traditionally a branch of evergreen, is nailed to the highest part of the roof structure as soon as it is reached. In many parts of the world the arrival at this stage of the building is a signal for much merrymaking.

ROSIN PAPER. see BUILDING PAPER

ROUGH OPENING

The rough openings are the spaces left in the framework of a wooden building or in the masonry of a brick building for the subsequent doors and windows.

ROUGH OPENINGS FOR
DOOR AND WINDOW
IN WOOD FRAMING

TWO-STORIED HOUSE   from PERSPECTIVA by HIERONIMUS RODLER,   1546

SADDLE

A saddle is the hardwood strip found at the bottom of a doorway between interior rooms. Its purpose is to cover the joint between the two rooms' floors.

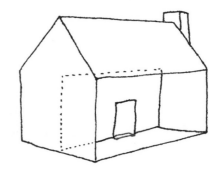

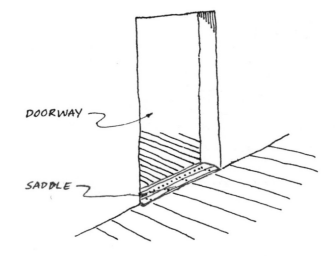

DOORWAY

SADDLE

SASH

Derived from the same word as chassis (which means frame), sash refers to the actual frame which holds the glass of a window. Strictly speaking, every window is comprised of a sash and a casing, but the term sash window generally refers to a window which slides up and down.

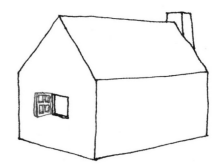

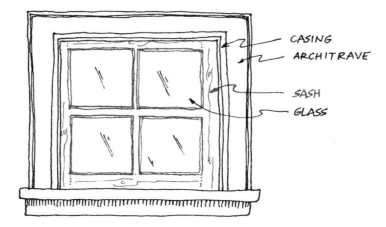

CASING
ARCHITRAVE

SASH
GLASS

SASH WEIGHT

Sash weights are the heavy pieces of metal used to counterbalance the sashes of double-hung windows. Attached to the actual sash by sash cord, the weights move up and down inside narrow boxes on either side of the window.

SASH WEIGHTS WITH WOVEN
SASH CORD (TO RESIST STRETCH)

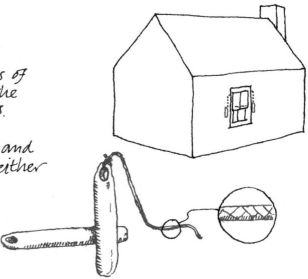

SCREEN

Screen windows or screen doors are window and door frames fitted with fine mesh screen to allow the passage of air but not of insects. Such doors and windows are used in addition to the regular doors and windows during warm weather (and in temperate areas are often exchanged for storm doors and windows during cold weather).

SEPTIC TANK

A septic tank is a large concrete or metal tank buried in the ground, which receives all the sewage of a house. It is so designed that the waste separates into sludge which sinks to the bottom and decomposes, and liquid which is drained off from the top of the tank into an underground leaching bed.

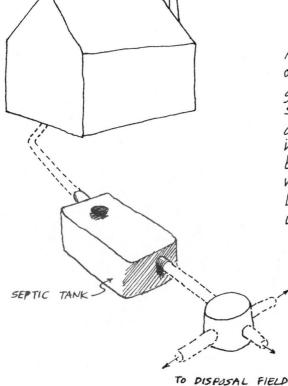

SEPTIC TANK

TO DISPOSAL FIELD

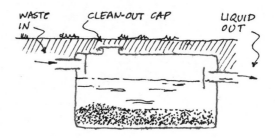

WASTE IN   CLEAN-OUT CAP   LIQUID OUT

147

SEWER

A sewer started off life, in the Middle Ages, as an overflow channel for a fishpond, but has since become rather less salubrious as an underground channel which collects and discharges all the waste water and refuse from a house. A sewer is generally part of a municipally owned system which serves many houses.

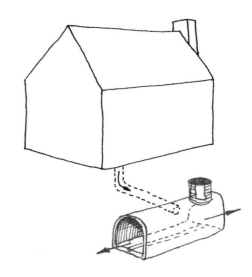

SHAKE

A shake is a piece of wood which has been cut by hand to form a roof shingle. Shakes are made from rot-resistant species of wood such as cedar. Commercially made shakes are normally sawn on one side and are thus known as resawn shakes.

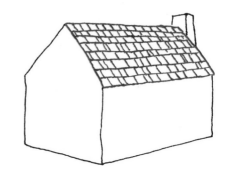

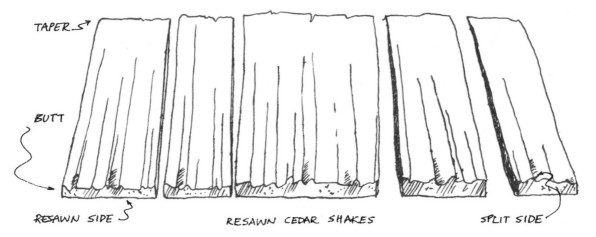

TAPER

BUTT

RESAWN SIDE

RESAWN CEDAR SHAKES

SPLIT SIDE

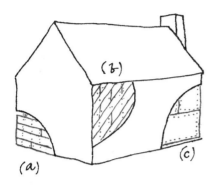

SHEATHING

The sheathing is the first skin or covering of a wood-frame house, over which the siding is subsequently fixed. Sheathing was at first either horizontal boards (as at (a)), or diagonal boards (as at (b)) which are stronger, but is now usually made of plywood (as at (c)) or sheets of some other semirigid insulating material.

SHED ROOF. see ROOF

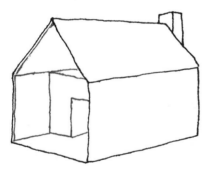

SHEETROCK
GYPSUM BOARD
PLASTERBOARD

Sheetrock, known in Britain as plasterboard, is now one of the commonest interior wall coverings. Essentially a sandwich of gypsum between two layers of paper, it is made in various thicknesses and sizes. It is easily cut, and when nailed in place its joints are hidden by 'taping' — a process of applying thin and narrow strips of paper and a special joint compound. Its chief virtue is that it is many times quicker than plaster in application, though for appearance it can never match plaster. Sheetrocked walls are often called drywall - in distinction to plaster walls which are wet when constructed.

SHINGLE

A shingle, which was originally only a small piece of thin wood, used as an overlapping roof covering, may now also be a thin piece of asbestos or asphalt, similarly used. Shakes are a thicker, handmade form of wood shingles.

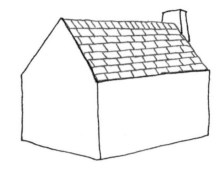

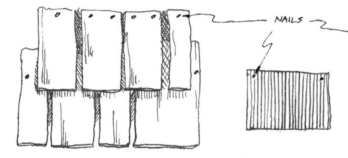

NAILS

WOOD SHINGLES   ASBESTOS SHINGLE   ASPHALT SHINGLES

SHINGLE MOULDING

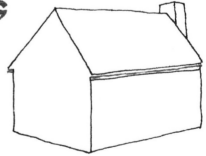

The shingle moulding is a strip of moulding fixed to the fascia of a cornice immediately below the bottom of the first row of roof shingles. For a detailed illustration see CROWN MOULDING. Shingle moulding is often dispensed with nowadays, and its place is largely taken by aluminum strips called drip edge (see DRIP EDGE).

SHUTTER

A shutter is a hinged door which covers a window. Very often just simple boards, shutters may also be quite complicated affairs which fold back into carefully made boxings. Shutters may be found on the inside or the outside.

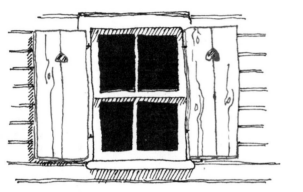

EXTERIOR SHUTTERS

INTERIOR BOXED SHUTTERS

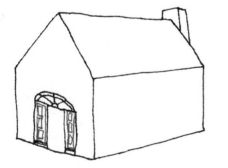

SIDELIGHT

The term sidelight refers to the narrow vertical windows found at the side of front entrance doors. These windows do not generally open, hence the use of the term 'light' which signifies just the pane of glass.

SIDING CLADDING

Unless the walls of a house are made with some integral material such as brick or stone, they will need to be covered, and all the various materials used for this purpose are known generically as siding, and in Britain as cladding. Illustrated below are some of the different kinds of siding in common use.

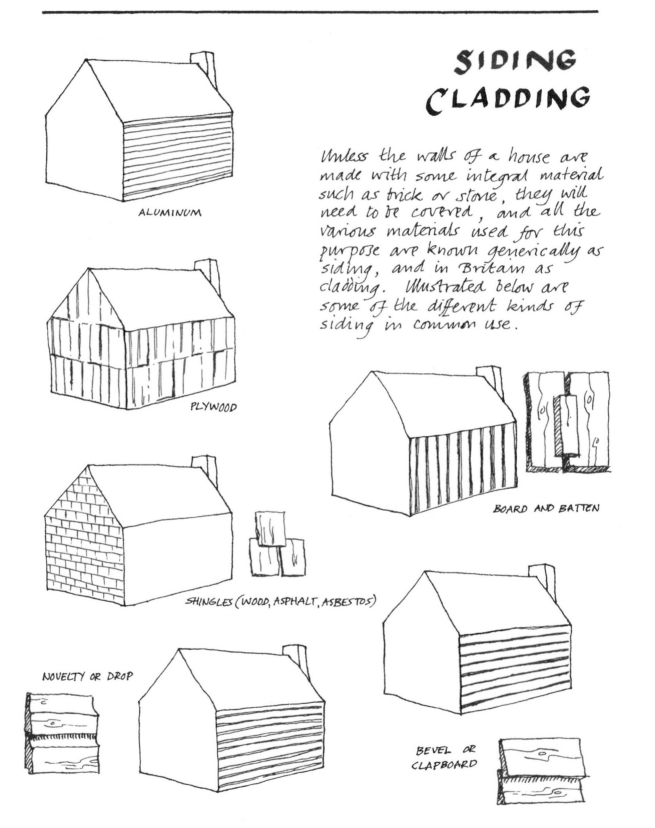

ALUMINUM

PLYWOOD

BOARD AND BATTEN

SHINGLES (WOOD, ASPHALT, ASBESTOS)

NOVELTY OR DROP

BEVEL OR CLAPBOARD

SILL
CILL

The sill is the horizontal piece of stone or wood at the bottom of a frame – whether it be the frame of a window, a door, or of a whole house.

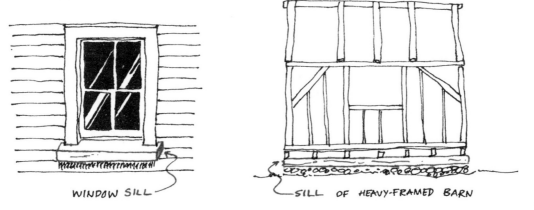

WINDOW SILL

SILL OF HEAVY-FRAMED BARN

SKIRTING or SKIRTINGBOARD.
see BASEBOARD

SKYLIGHT

A skylight is a window in the roof of a house, which may or may not open, but which by definition is slanting or horizontal and never vertical. The skylight is used for top lighting, as of a stairwell or attic.

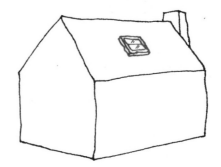

SLAB

Slab is the term used to describe
a flat bed of concrete on which
a house is sometimes built. Slabs
are often constructed on the
surface rather than being poured
into an excavated hole; the
weight of the house is evenly
distributed over the whole area
covered by the slab, and the need
for a dug foundation obviated.

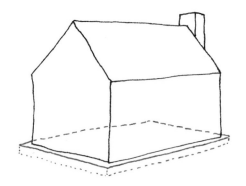

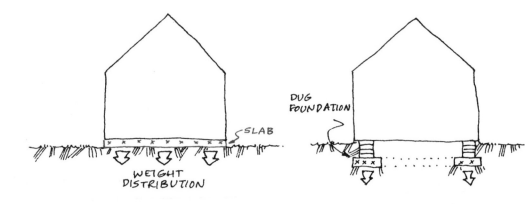

SLAB

WEIGHT
DISTRIBUTION

DUG
FOUNDATION

SLATE

A slate is a thin rectangular piece
of stone used as an overlapping
roof covering, more common in
Britain than in America

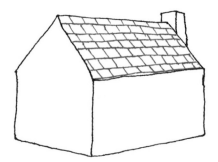

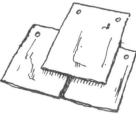

154

SLEEPER

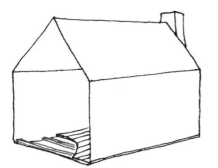

A sleeper is a horizontal timber on which joists (the timbers which support a floor) are laid. Sleepers, which were originally called ground joists, are also used on concrete floors when a wooden floor is to be superimposed.

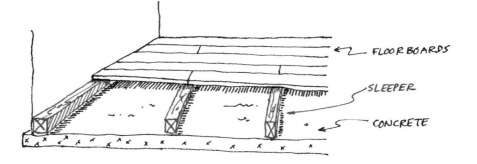

FLOOR BOARDS

SLEEPER

CONCRETE

SMOKE CHAMBER

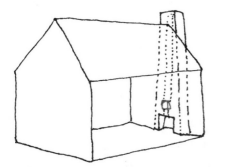

The smoke chamber is the enlarged area between the bottom of the flue and the top of the throat — the opening in the top of a fireplace made narrow by the smoke shelf, in order to prevent downdrafts.

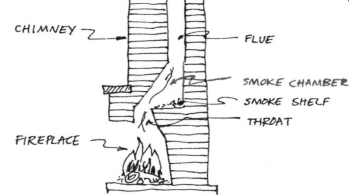

CHIMNEY

FLUE

SMOKE CHAMBER

SMOKE SHELF

THROAT

FIREPLACE

CROSS-SECTION OF FIREPLACE

155

SOFFIT

Soffit is a word which means the visible horizontal underside of something - such as a lintel, a staircase, a beam, or a roof overhang. However, its most common application in a house is referring to the board forming the bottom of a roof overhang cornice.

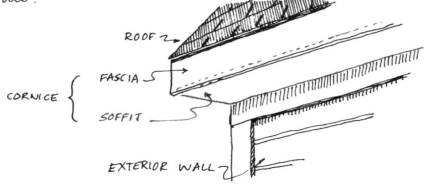

ROOF

FASCIA

CORNICE {

SOFFIT

EXTERIOR WALL

SOIL PIPE

The soil pipe is the main drainpipe, usually made of cast iron, into which all the other waste pipes lead, and which in turn, empties either into the house's own, or the town's sewage system.

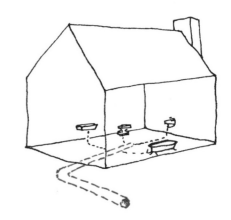

SOLE PLATE. see PLATE

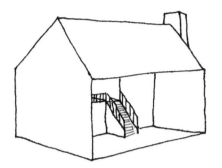

STAIR

A stair is a step, but it is generally used in the plural to signify a succession of steps, arranged between two points at different levels in a house. Stairs are further distinguished by their design, such as circular, dog-legged, elliptic, etc.

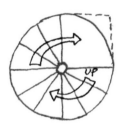

CIRCULAR OR SPIRAL STAIRS

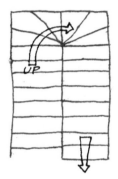

DOG-LEGGED STAIRS

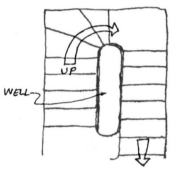

WELL

WELL STAIRS

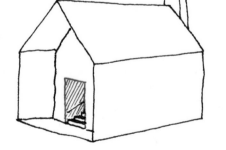

STAIRCASE

The staircase is the space or enclosure occupied by stairs and landings, although it is often improperly used to mean the stairs themselves.

STAIRWELL

The stairwell is the space occupied by a flight of stairs; the well hole is the opening in the floor at the top of a flight of stairs.

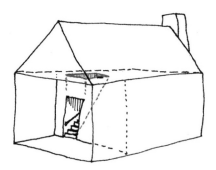

STEP

A step is one of the footspaces or platforms in a flight of stairs. In wooden stairs the step usually consists of a riser and a tread. There are various kinds of steps built for different types of stairs.

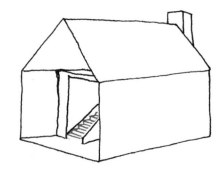

DIFFERENT KINDS OF STEP

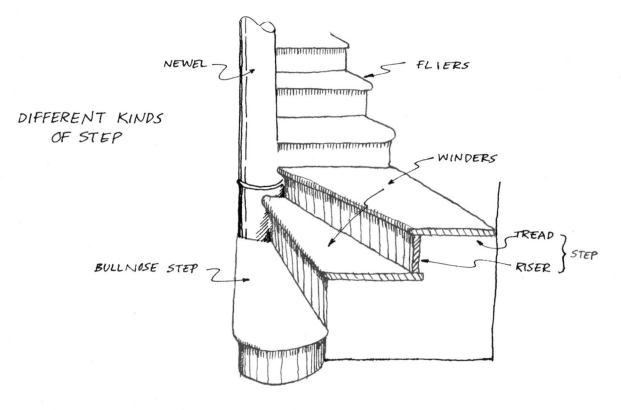

NEWEL

FLIERS

WINDERS

TREAD

RISER

} STEP

BULLNOSE STEP

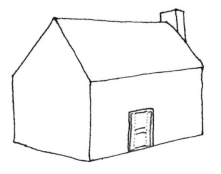

STILE

A stile is a vertical piece in a frame – such as the stile of a door or a window – which holds the horizontal pieces at top and bottom known as rails. (The intermediate vertical members sometimes found in doors and other framework do not hold the rails but rather are themselves held by the rails – and are called muntins.)

FRAMEWORK OF A PANELED DOOR

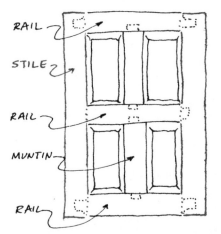

RAIL

STILE

RAIL

MUNTIN

RAIL

STOOL

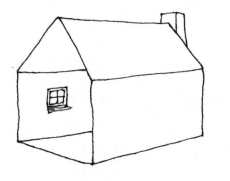

The stool is the horizontal shelf at the bottom of a window on the inside.

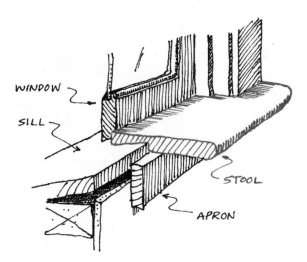

WINDOW

SILL

STOOL

APRON

STOOP

Stoop, which comes from the same Dutch word as step, is used chiefly in North America to indicate the steps leading up to the front door of a house.

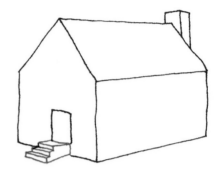

STOP

A stop is a piece of wood nailed to the inside of a door or window frame (properly called the casing) to form the recess against which the door or window shuts.

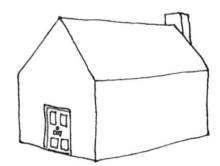

In older work (and now with metal door frames) the stop was often an integral part of the actual casing, being cut from the solid wood.

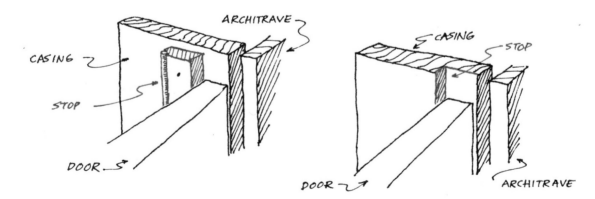

SEPARATE AND INTEGRAL DOOR STOPS

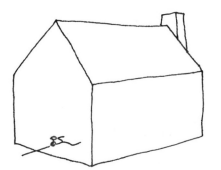

STOPCOCK

A stopcock, often called more obviously a shutoff valve in America, is a tap or short pipe fitted with a device whereby the flow of the contents of the pipe may be shut off. Stopcocks are commonly found in the water, gas, and oil lines of a house.

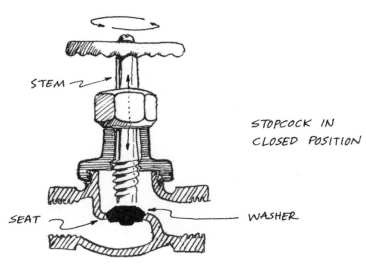

STEM

STOPCOCK IN CLOSED POSITION

SEAT

WASHER

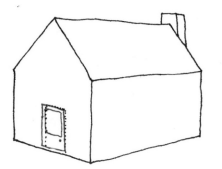

STORM DOOR

A storm door is an extra door fitted to an exterior door to provide added protection from cold weather. Actually, exterior doors should be insulated anyway, but summer screen doors are often converted to storm doors by the addition of a panel of glass.

STORM WINDOW

Of more value than storm doors, storm windows consist of a second sash fitted into a window thereby providing double glazing and better insulation against cold weather. Often interchangeable with screen windows for summer use, storm windows are less convenient than windows actually fitted with two layers of glass. The two layers trap a dead air space which provides an insulated barrier against heat transference.

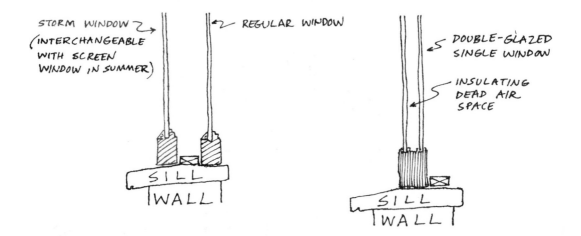

STORM WINDOW
(INTERCHANGEABLE WITH SCREEN WINDOW IN SUMMER)

REGULAR WINDOW

SILL
WALL

DOUBLE-GLAZED SINGLE WINDOW

INSULATING DEAD AIR SPACE

SILL
WALL

STOREY

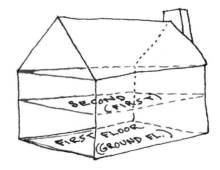

The various levels of a building are called stories. The American first floor is the British ground floor; the first floor in Britain is thus the second floor in America.

SECOND (FIRST)

FIRST FLOOR (GROUND FL.)

162

STRINGER

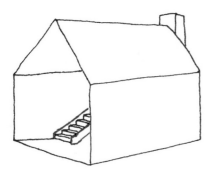

stringers (also called strings and string boards) are the sloping boards which hold the ends of the steps of a set of stairs.

Stringers may be open or closed. When a staircase is built against a wall, the stringer next the wall is known as the wall stringer; the outside stringer as the outer stringer.

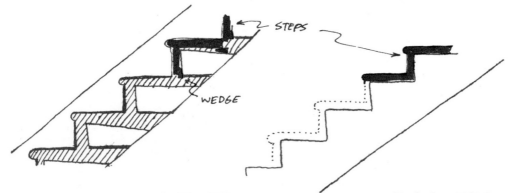

CLOSED STRINGER SHOWING GROOVES CUT TO RECEIVE THE ENDS OF THE STEPS WHICH ARE HELD IN PLACE WITH WEDGES

OPEN STRINGER SHOWING HOW STEPS REST ON STRINGER

STRUCTURAL INSULATING BOARD

Structural insulating board is made of large sheets of semi-rigid material with good insulating properties. It is used as sheathing for a wood-framed house (the first covering, over which the siding is nailed) although sheets of plywood are generally relied upon at the corners to provide the requisite strength to the frame.

STRUT

A strut is strictly any piece of timber in a system of framing which is pressed in the direction of its length. The commonest strut in a house is that found in some kinds of roofs, connecting tie beams to rafters, etc.

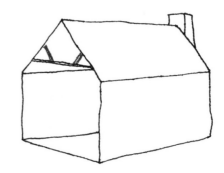

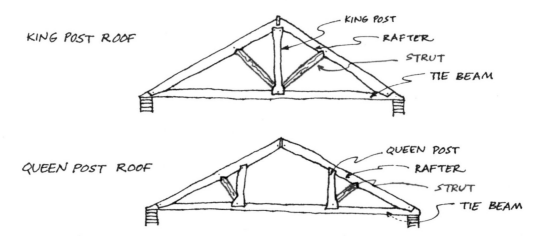

KING POST ROOF

KING POST
RAFTER
STRUT
TIE BEAM

QUEEN POST ROOF

QUEEN POST
RAFTER
STRUT
TIE BEAM

STUCCO

Stucco, which actually means any kind of plasterwork, is generally used to refer to an outside covering of cement. Exterior walls are sometimes stuccoed with pebbledash — a mixture of cement and fine stones.

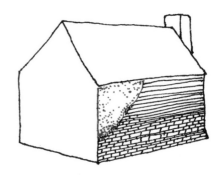

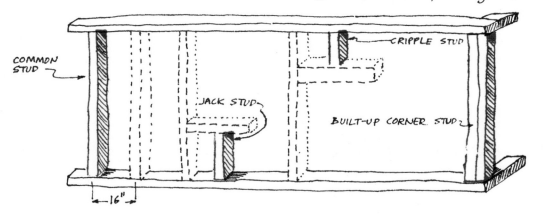

STUD

Studs are the upright framing members of a house. Once called quarters, much larger, and spaced further apart, common studs are now approximately 2"×4" (50mm × 100mm) and placed 16" (400mm) apart.

Studs may be classified according to their position and length, such as gable, corner, and jack stud.

CRIPPLE STUD

COMMON STUD

JACK STUD

BUILT-UP CORNER STUD

16"

STUMP. see PIER

SUB-FLOOR

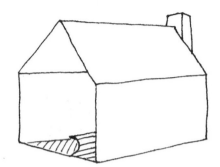

Well-constructed houses are made with two floors — a sub-floor and a finish floor. The sub-floor, which is now usually plywood, but previously consisted of boards laid diagonally (or at least at right angles) to the finish floor, provides more stability and stiffness, and allows an intermediate layer of insulating board or building paper to be used, which acts as a dust barrier in the event of any shrinkage of the floor boards.

Some buildings, which are designed to be carpeted have only one floor (usually made from sheets of particleboard) over which the carpet is laid directly. Although this is the only floor, it is not really a finish floor, and so must also be called a sub-floor.

SUMMER BEAM

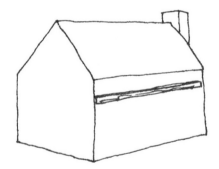

The term summer beam is a redundancy, since summer means beam. What is meant is breastsummer (see BREASTSUMMER).

SUMP

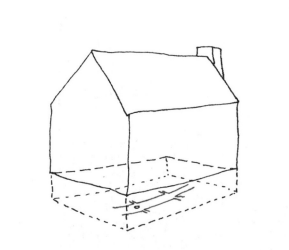

A sump (which derives from swamp) is a pit or hole in a basement designed to collect any water, and from which, by means of a sump pump, such water is drained.

SWALE

A swale is a wide but shallow trench sometimes dug in unfinished basements to drain any water which might collect (usually into a sump, whence it could be pumped out).

HEAVY TIMBER FRAMING   *from* PERSPECTIVA *by* HIERONIMVS RODLER,   1546

TAIL
CREEPER

A certain amount of confusion exists about the terms 'tail' and 'creeper' because they can mean the same thing or two different things. In the sense that tail is sometimes used in American for the more correct term 'lookout,' creeper may be considered the British equivalent. However, tail more properly refers (on both sides of the Atlantic, to the end of a rafter overhanging the wall plate on which the rafter rests.

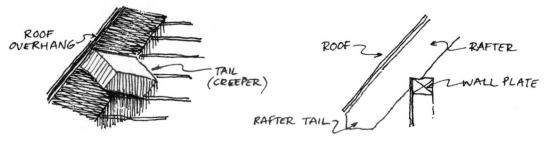

ROOF OVERHANG

TAIL (CREEPER)

ROOF

RAFTER

RAFTER TAIL

WALL PLATE

TAR PAPER. see BUILDING PAPER

TERMITE SHIELD

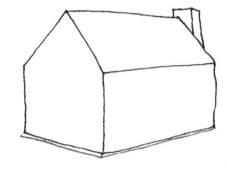

Termites are a serious problem in many parts of America and wooden houses must be constructed with a termite shield around the top of the foundation to prevent termites from attacking the wood structure.

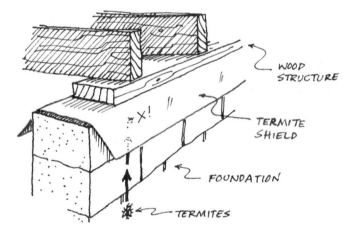

SHOWING HOW TERMITES CRAWL UP FOUNDATION BUT CANNOT PENETRATE METAL TERMITE SHIELD

WOOD STRUCTURE

TERMITE SHIELD

FOUNDATION

TERMITES

TERRACE

A terrace is a raised area around a house – not to be confused with a deck, which is a raised area over the ground; a porch or veranda, which has a roof; or a patio, which is similar but which is not raised.

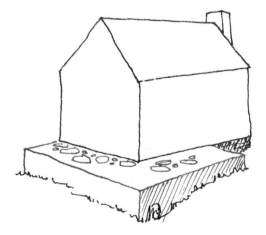

THERMOSTAT

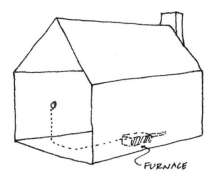
— FURNACE

A common feature in houses with some kind of central heating, the thermostat is an automatic device that regulates the amount of heat produced by being set to a predetermined temperature.

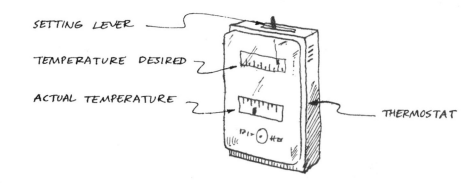

SETTING LEVER

TEMPERATURE DESIRED

ACTUAL TEMPERATURE

THERMOSTAT

THRESHOLD

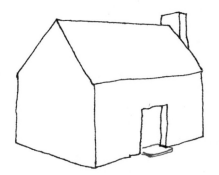

The threshold symbolizes the entry to a house by virtue of it being the stone or timber forming the bottom of a doorway, over which one must cross to enter the house.

It is derived not from being the place where grain was threshed, but rather from a Saxon word meaning 'across', from which is also derived the modern word 'through.'

TIE BEAM

A tie beam is a horizontal timber that 'ties' the bottom of a pair of rafters together. It should not be confused with a collar beam, which is placed higher up, since these beams have opposite purposes. The tie beam is under tension, preventing the feet of the rafters from spreading outwards, while the collar beam is in a state of compression, resisting the inward thrust of the rafters.

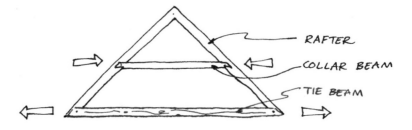

RAFTER
COLLAR BEAM
TIE BEAM

TILE

There are three kinds of tile used in a house: **1.** a thin unglazed slab of baked clay used as a roof covering; **2.** a thin, glazed, and often decorated tile for lining walls and floors (many other materials are used in this form); **3.** a curved or tube-like piece of clay used for subterranean drainage, and in baked form as a chimney lining.

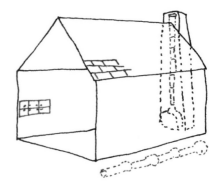

TILTING FILLET

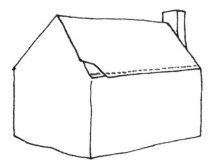

A tilting fillet is a fillet of wood with one edge thicker than the other, laid under slates or tiles at the edge of a roof in order to raise them slightly.

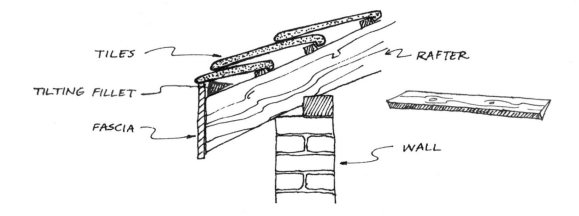

TILES

TILTING FILLET

FASCIA

RAFTER

WALL

TOE PLATE, TOP PLATE. see PLATE

TRANSOM

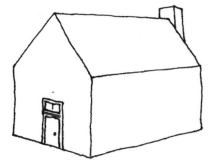

Transom means originally a timber or stone that spans an opening and supports a superstructure. Its use and size has shrunk, however, and now chiefly refers to a bar across a window, or across the top of a door with a small window above. (This window is often referred to as the transom (window).)

TRAP

A trap is a bend in the drainpipe of a water fixture (such as a sink or a bathtub), which holds water in order to form a barrier to sewer gases which might otherwise rise up into the house.

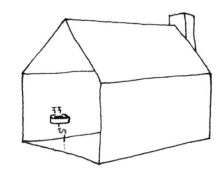

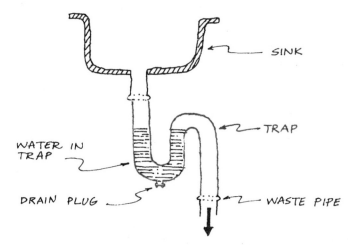

SINK

TRAP

WATER IN TRAP

DRAIN PLUG

WASTE PIPE

TRAPDOOR

A trapdoor is a door which is flush with the surface of a floor or a ceiling, and which is used to provide access to basements, crawl spaces, or attics.

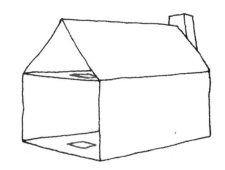

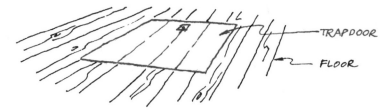

TRAPDOOR

FLOOR

TREAD

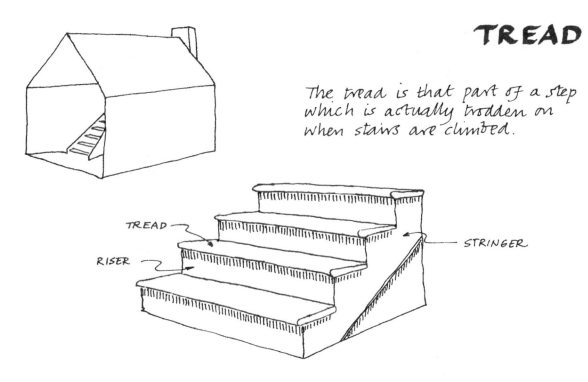

The tread is that part of a step which is actually trodden on when stairs are climbed.

TREAD

RISER

STRINGER

TRIM

Trim is the name given to all the woodwork in a house which finishes doorways, windows, edges, and corners. A rather loose term, it is difficult to determine where 'structural' carpentry ends and 'trim' or 'finish' carpentry begins. A door, for example, is said to be 'trimmed out' when, having been hung in its casing, the architrave and moulding is fixed in place, even though the architrave has the structural effect of helping hold the casing in place.

175

TRIMMER

A trimmer is a doubled, or extra thick, joist or rafter found at the side of an opening in the floor or the roof. Its purpose is to provide the extra strength necessitated by the opening.

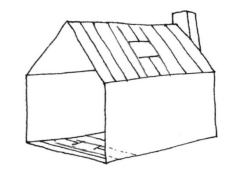

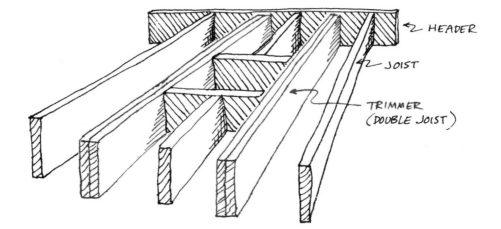

HEADER

JOIST

TRIMMER (DOUBLE JOIST)

TRUSS

A truss in a building is a system of beams so arranged as to span an opening and be self-supporting. The commonest trusses are those made to support roofs, but floors are sometimes supported by trusses too. (See illustration facing page 95.)

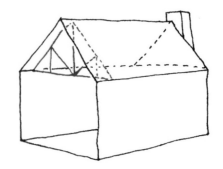

176

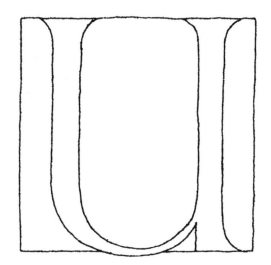

UNDERLAYMENT

Underlayment is anything that
is laid under something else.
Specifically, in a house, underlayment can refer to a roof
covering (usually of building
paper) put down before the roof
shingles are applied (to more
completely seal and waterproof
the roof), or to a smooth underfloor laid down as a base for
tiles or linoleum (in this case the underlayment often consists
of smooth plywood or Masonite).

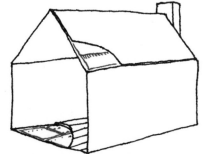

FLOOR TILES

UNDERLAYMENT

JOISTS

177

TWO MONKS BUILDING THEIR CHAPEL   a woodcut by MICHAEL FURTER, 1496

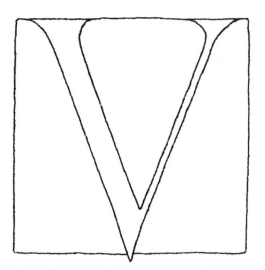

VALLEY

A valley is the internal angle formed by two roof slopes meeting with their axis at right angles.

AXIS 2

VALLEY

VALLEY BOARD

A valley board is a flat board which lies in the bottom of a valley between two roof slopes. Its purpose is to form the base for a valley gutter.

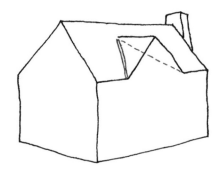

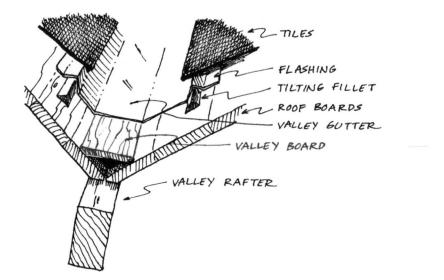

TILES

FLASHING
TILTING FILLET
ROOF BOARDS
VALLEY GUTTER
VALLEY BOARD

VALLEY RAFTER

VAPOR BARRIER

A vapor barrier is commonly created by a continuous sheet of plastic behind the walls and ceilings of a house. The purpose of such a barrier is to prevent moisture from the house's interior condensing in the walls and roof and leading to rot

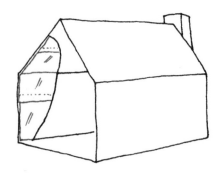

VENETIAN WINDOW. see WINDOW

VENT

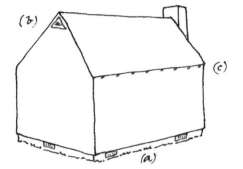

There are, or should be in a properly constructed house, many vents, the function of which is to ventilate areas susceptible to dampness or condensation, and so prevent rot and decay. Some of the necessary vents are basement or foundation vents (a), attic and roof vents (b), and eave vents (c).

VENT PIPE
VENT STACK

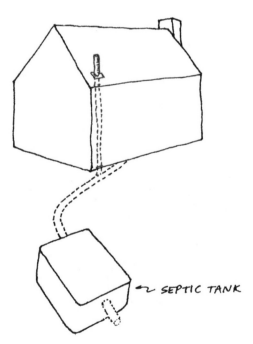

SEPTIC TANK

The vent pipe or vent stack is an escape pipe for sewer gases which might otherwise back up into the house. However, seeking the easiest way up, they escape up the vent pipe which rises above the house

VERANDA

The word veranda, sometimes spelt with a terminal 'h', came into English, via India, from Portuguese, and signifies an open gallery alongside a house, with its own roof. In America, the tendency is to call this place the porch, although a porch is strictly a covered entrance way.

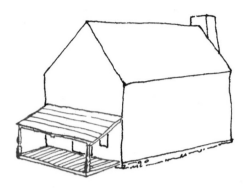

VERGEBOARD. see BARGEBOARD

WAINSCOT

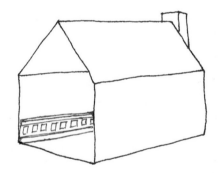

Wainscot meant originally the woodwork which framed the sides of a wain or wagon; then the kind of wood (chiefly oak, imported to England from the Baltic countries) used for this kind of work; and finally the half-paneling of a room - made from the same kind of wood.

PLASTER

WALL

WAINSCOT

WALING

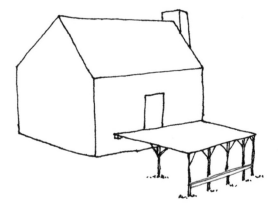

A waling is a horizontal strut used to connect a row of wooden posts, as might support a deck or veranda.

WALL

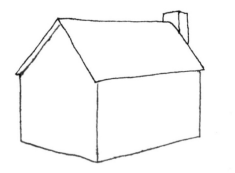

It is walls which make a house, and as such they may be distinguished by purpose, such as bearing walls, which support higher floors and roofs; curtain walls and partition walls which support no weight but divide areas; or retaining walls, whose function is to hold back the earth. Walls may also be classified ad infinitum by construction, for example, single walls, double walls, cavity walls, interior walls, exterior walls, wood walls, stone walls, brick walls, etc.

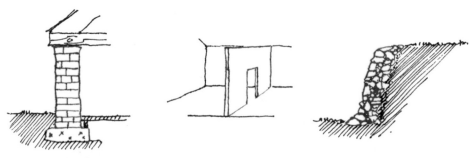

BEARING (FOUNDATION) WALL   PARTITION WALL   RETAINING WALL

WATERTABLE

The watertable is a protruding drip edge built around the bottom of a wood-sided house. The watertable not only gives the bottom of the siding a neat finish but by allowing the water to drip off away from the building, helps prevent rot, especially to the bottom of the siding.

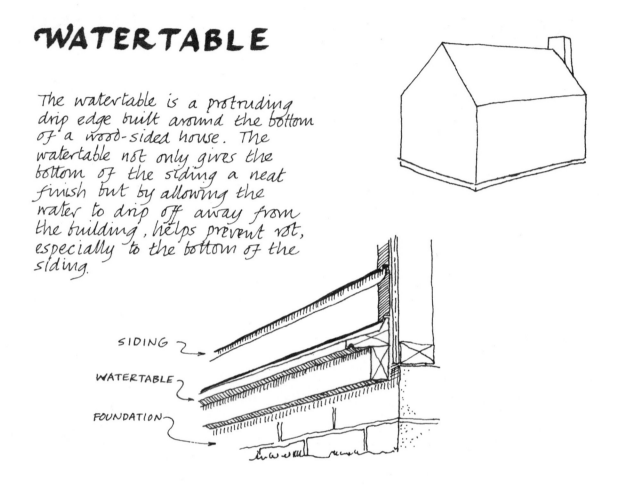

SIDING
WATERTABLE
FOUNDATION

WEATHERHEAD

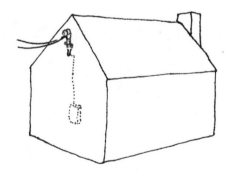

The weatherhead is the metal fitting attached high up on the outside of a house to which outside power lines are connected (unless, of course, the electricity is brought underground to the house).

WELL

Many houses which have their own water supply, obtain it from a well — essentially a deep hole in the ground from which water is drawn or pumped. The other common source is surface water such as a stream or a spring — which is what the word well originally meant, though it has now sunk underground.

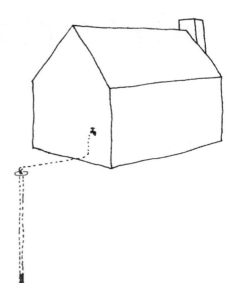

WICKET

A wicket is a small entrance door constructed in a larger door or gate.

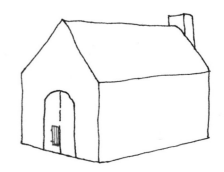

WIDOW'S WALK

A widow's walk is an observation platform on the roof of a house, typically that of a New England sailor's house, from where the possible widow could watch for the arrival of her husband's ship.

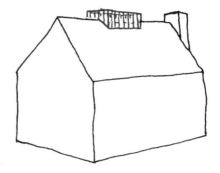

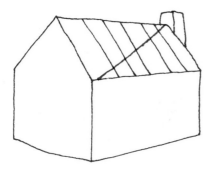

WIND BEAM

A diagonal roof beam, laid from the foot of one rafter to the head of another, is called a wind beam. The purpose of the wind beam is to provide a brace against the racking or winding of the roof. This is achieved nowadays with the use of plywood sheathing.

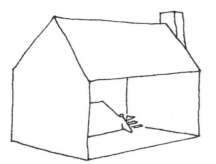

WINDER

Winder is the name given to an irregularly shaped step in a flight of stairs which turns a corner or winds around a newel post. (A straight step is called a flier.)

WINDERS

FLIERS

UP

PLAN OF
DOG-LEGGED
STAIRCASE

SPIRAL STAIRCASE

WINDOW

The word window meant 'wind eye' in Saxon, and was simply a hole in the roof through which smoke from the fire could escape. Nowadays, windows are commonly glazed and used for letting in light. There are numerous designs of windows, some of which are illustrated below.

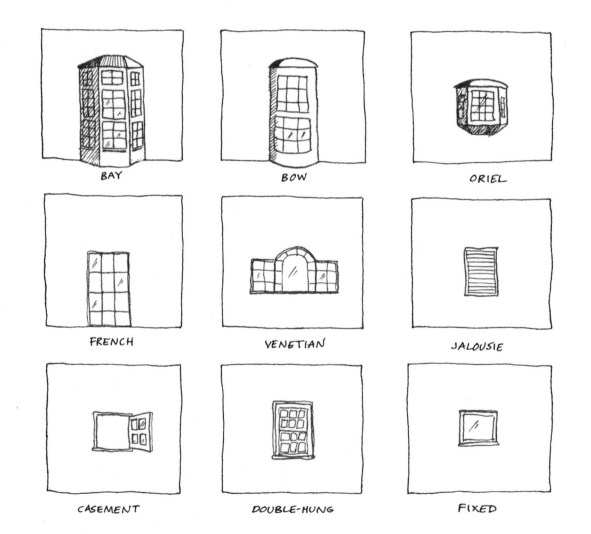

BAY

BOW

ORIEL

FRENCH

VENETIAN

JALOUSIE

CASEMENT

DOUBLE-HUNG

FIXED

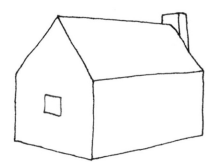

WINDOW FRAME

The term window frame, though common, is vague since it can mean either the casing, in which the window sash is hung, or the sash itself which holds the glass. Both parts are popularly referred to as the window frame.

CASING   SASH

WINDOW SILL

Window sill is used to mean the bottom parts of a window opening, both inside and outside. The inside sill often forms a flat shelf, but the outside part is usually a sloping area. The inside part is properly called the stool. (See **APRON** for an illustration of both parts.)

189

WIRE LATH

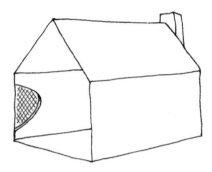

Wire Lath is the modern means of fixing plaster to a wall or ceiling. Instead of the older method of plastering onto narrowly spaced strips of wood called laths, a sheet of stamped-out wire mesh is used which holds the plaster much better and which also affords more integral strength to the plaster (see LATH).

WIRING

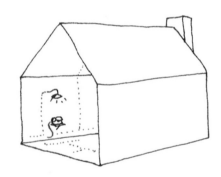

There is much wiring in a modern house, most of which is hidden in the walls, floors, and ceilings. There may be several different systems — for electricity, for telephones, for electronic equipment such as radios, televisions, and record players, for thermostats, and for burglary detection devices — all of which may be collectively referred to as the wiring.

YOKE

Yoke is the correct name for the top part of a double-hung window casing (otherwise known as the head jamb).

OUTSIDE

YOKE

SASH PULLEY

PARTING STRIP

INSIDE

CROSS-SECTION THROUGH
DOUBLE-HUNG WINDOW

BELMONT COLLEGE LIBRARY

191

THE END